Picturing Polygons

2-D GEOMETRY

TERC

Investigations in Number, Data, and Space®

Dale Seymour Publications®

Menlo Park, California

The *Investigations* curriculum was developed at TERC (formerly Technical Education Research Centers) in collaboration with Kent State University and the State University of New York at Buffalo. The work was supported in part by National Science Foundation Grant No. ESI-9050210. TERC is a nonprofit company working to improve mathematics and science education. TERC is located at 2067 Massachusetts Avenue, Cambridge, MA 02140.

This project was supported, in part, by the
National Science Foundation
Opinions expressed are those of the authors and not necessarily those of the Foundation

Managing Editor: Catherine Anderson
Series Editor: Beverly Cory
Manuscript Editor: Karen Becker
ESL Consultant: Nancy Sokol Green
Production/Manufacturing Director: Janet Yearian
Production/Manufacturing Coordinator: Barbara Atmore
Design Manager: Jeff Kelly
Design: Don Taka
Illustrations: DJ Simison, Carl Yoshihara
Composition: Archetype Book Composition

This book is published by Dale Seymour Publications®, an imprint of Addison Wesley Longman, Inc.

Dale Seymour Publications
2725 Sand Hill Road
Menlo Park, CA 94025
Customer Service: 800-872-1100

DALE SEYMOUR PUBLICATIONS®

Order number DS47053
ISBN 1-57232-806-1
1 2 3 4 5 6 7 8 9 10-ML-01 00 99 98 97

Printed on Recycled Paper

Contents

*Repeated-use sheet

*Repeated-use sheet

Name Date

Student Sheet 1

Is It a Polygon?

1.

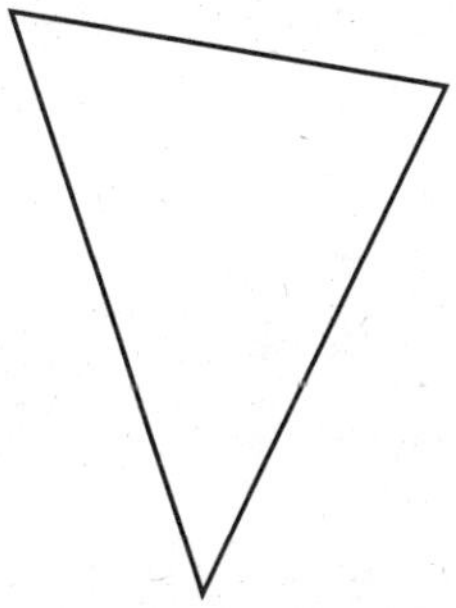

2.

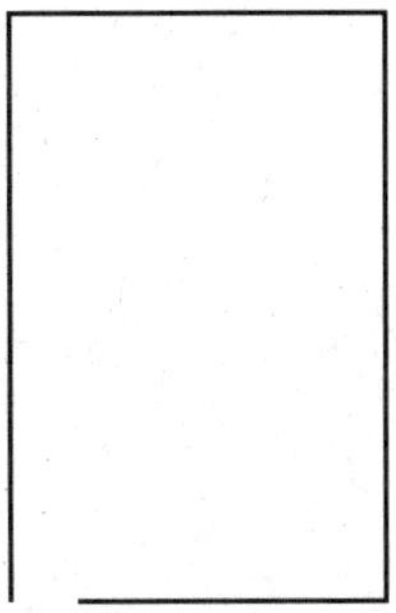

3.

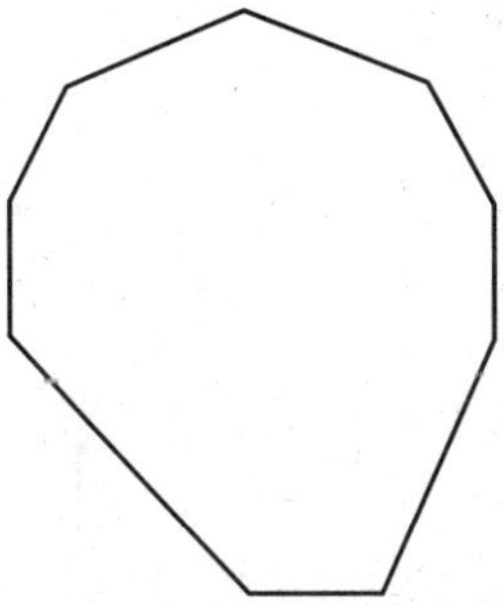

4.

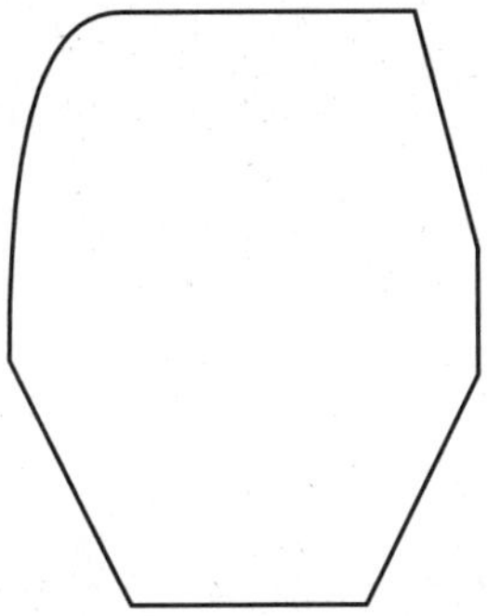

5.

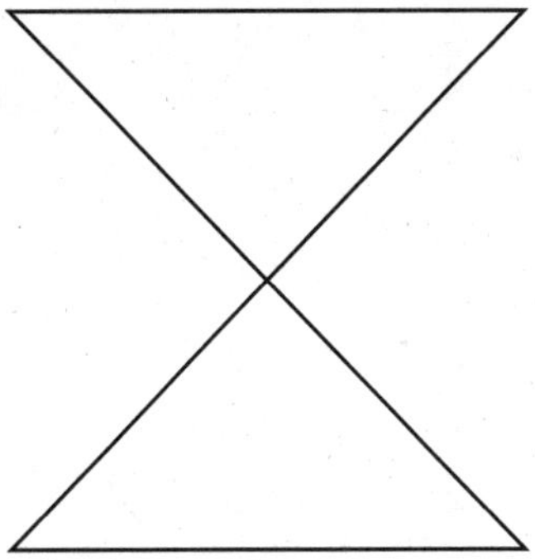

6.

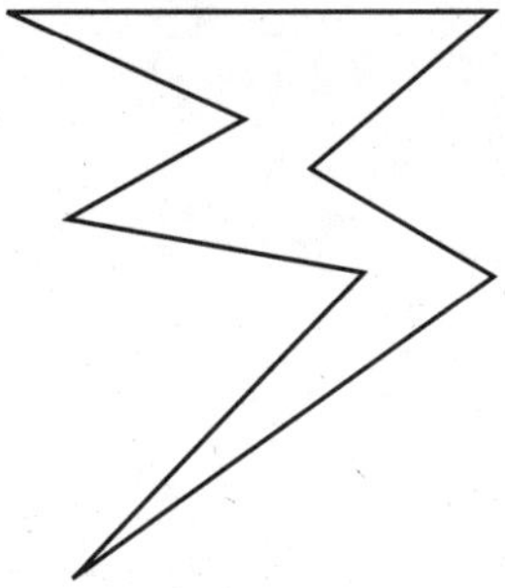

7.

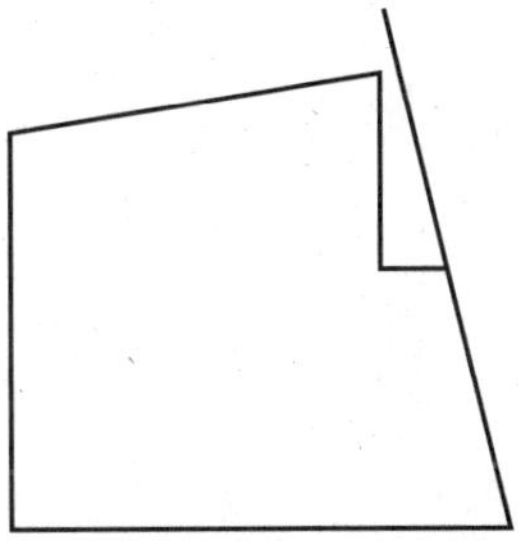

8.

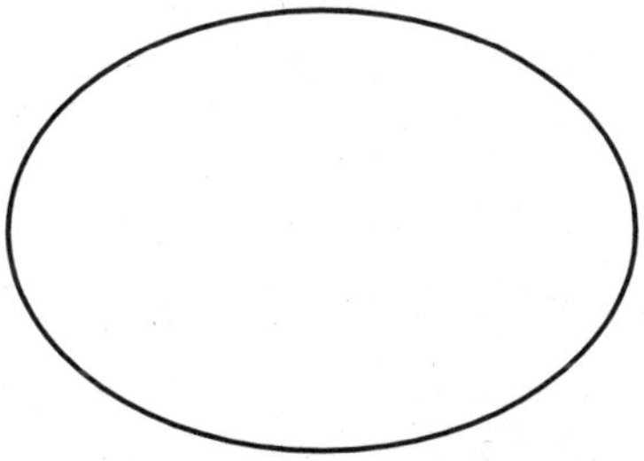

9.

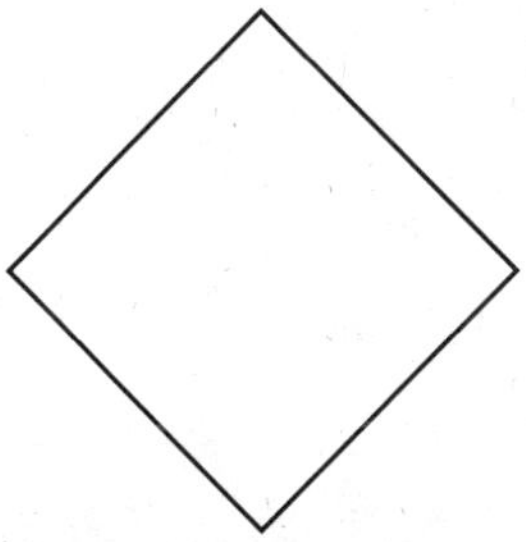

10.

11.

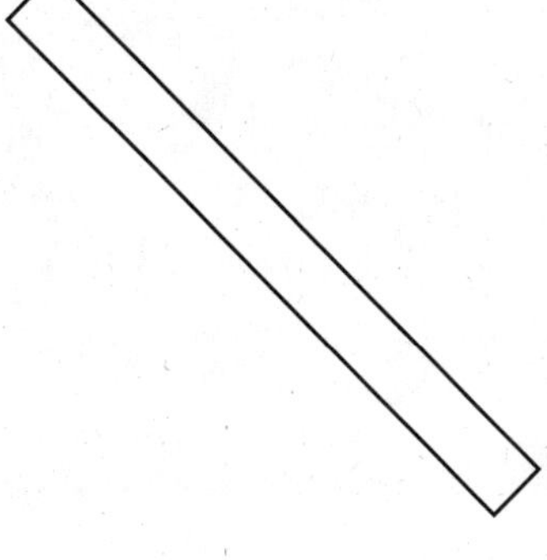

12.

Name Date

Student Sheet 2

Picasso's Polygons

How many polygons can you find in this drawing?

Make your own picture using **only** polygons.

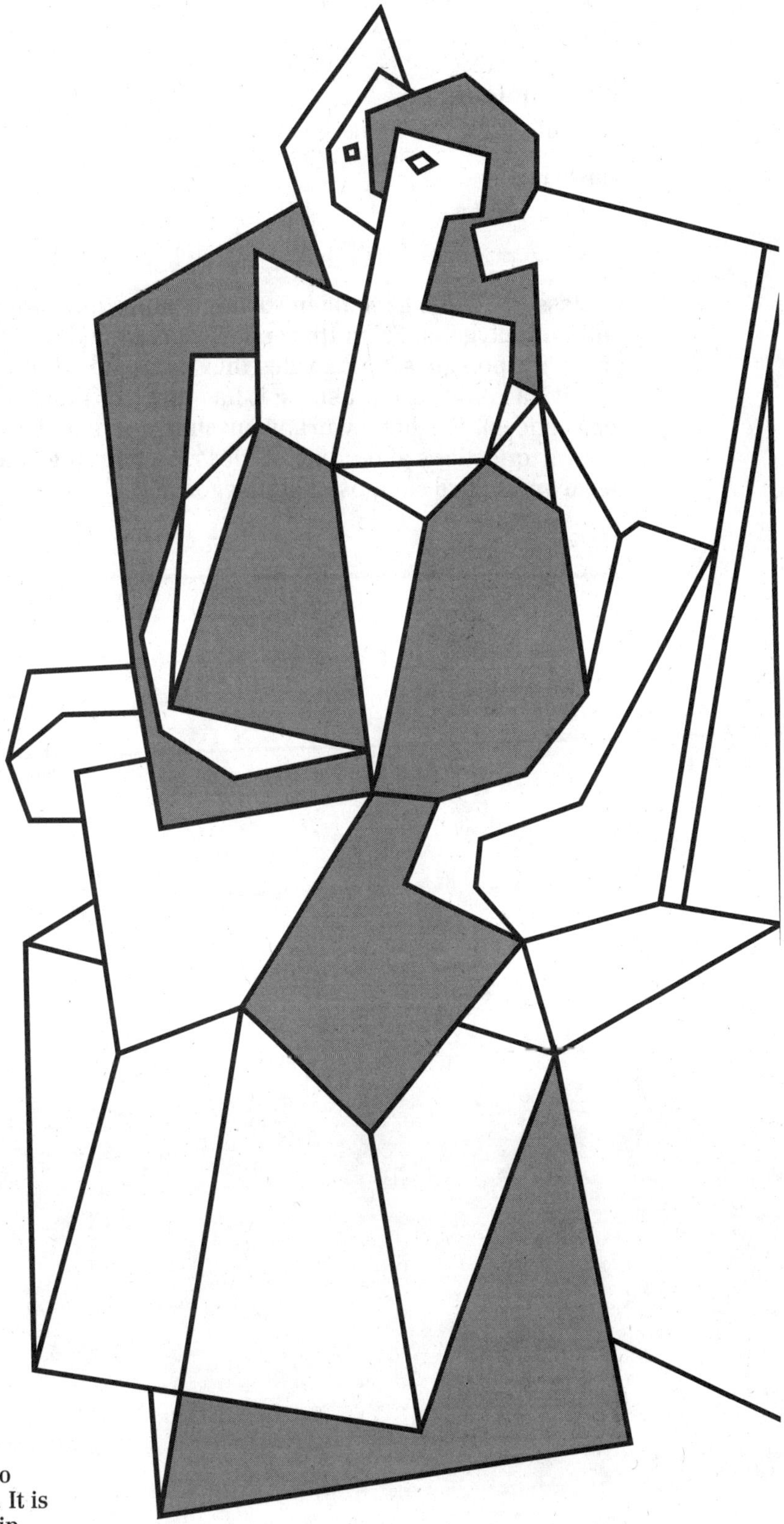

This figure is based on a pencil drawing by Pablo Picasso, *Woman in an Armchair,* Biarritz (1918). It is not a reproduction, but an illustration of the main polygonal forms in the drawing. Adaptation used by permission. Copyright © 1997 Estate of Pablo Picasso/Artists Rights Society (ARS), New York.

To the Family

Picasso's Polygons

Session 1

Math Content
Drawing polygons by using class definitions

Materials
Student Sheet 2
Pencil

In class, students have been sorting shapes into two categories: polygons and nonpolygons. From this experience, they developed their own definition for polygons. Some rules they came up with to define a polygon are: It has only straight sides; it has three or more sides; it has corners (or vertices). For homework, your child will use this information to answer questions about one of Picasso's paintings and to draw his or her own picture composed of polygons.

Name Date

Student Sheet 3

Coordinate Grids

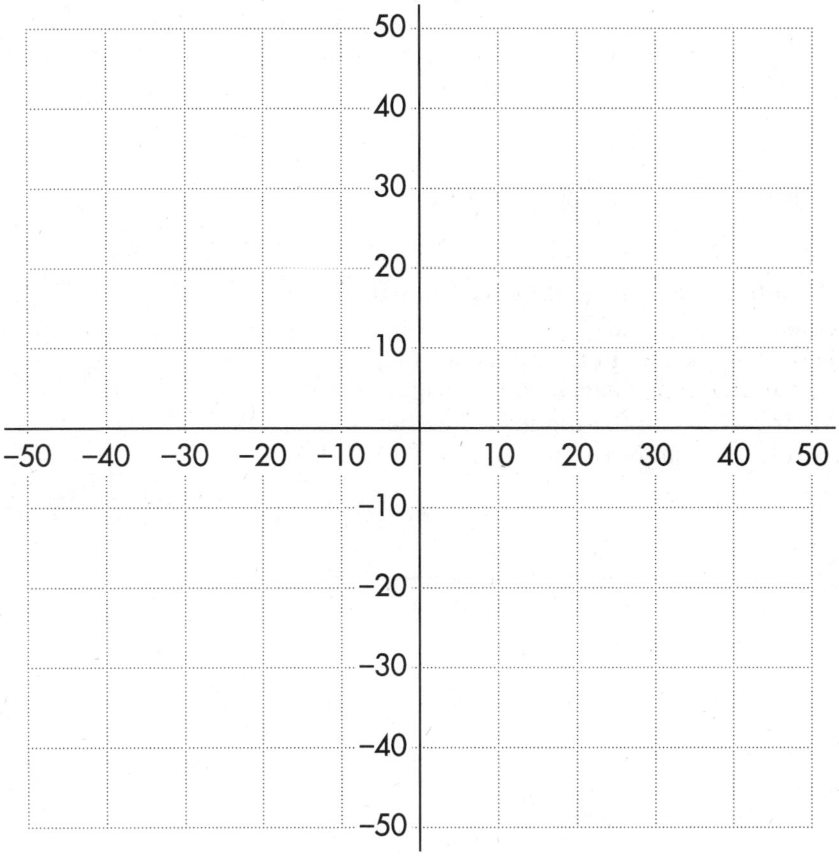

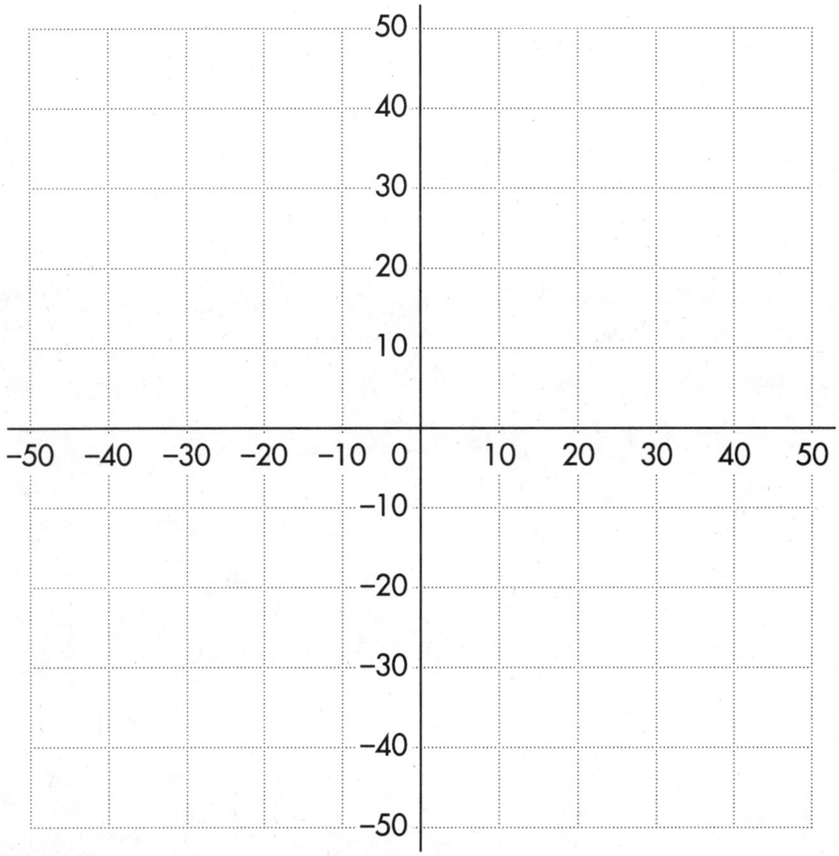

To the Family

Coordinate Grids

Session 2

Math Content
Locating points on a coordinate grid

Materials
Student Sheet 3
Pencil

For homework, your child will continue to work with polygons, using a coordinate grid to draw a simple polygon picture. All of the polygon's corners (or vertices) should be drawn on the intersections of the grid (or where the lines that form the individual squares on the grid paper meet). Students should draw their picture on the top grid. The bottom grid will be used in class tomorrow. You might remind your child to take this sheet to school tomorrow.

Name Date

Student Sheet 5

Types of Polygons

Fill in the second column of this chart with the name of the polygon for each number of sides.

Fill in the third column with related words or objects that use the same prefix (e.g., tri- for triangles).

Write on the back of the sheet any objects you see around you or know of that are examples of these polygons.

Number of sides	Name of polygon	Related words or objects
3		
4		
5		
6		
7		
8		
9		
10		
11		
12		

To the Family

Types of Polygons

Session 4

Math Content
Understanding the meaning of the prefixes used to identify polygons

Materials
Student Sheet 5
Dictionary
Pencil

In class, we listed names of polygons with the number of sides ranging from three to twelve. For homework, your child will look for words that have the same prefix as the polygon names and write the meaning of these words. Students will also list objects with polygon shapes on a separate piece of paper. You might help your child use the dictionary to look up related words or try to think of objects that are shaped like each polygon.

How to Get Started

- Open *Geo-Logo* with a double-click on the icon.
- Single-click the opening screen when instructed.
- Single-click an activity.

Geo-Logo Commands

`setxy [10 -20]` sets coordinates (10, –20)

`jumpto [-10 15]` moves turtle to (–10, 15)
Can be abbreviated `jt [-10 15]`

`fd 30` moves forward 30 turtle steps

`bk 12` moves back 12 turtle steps

`lt 90` turns left 90 degrees

`rt 60` turns right 60 degrees

`repeat 3 [fd 20 rt 90]` repeats the commands in brackets 3 times

`ht` hides turtle (`st` shows turtle)

`pu` puts pen up (`pd` puts pen down)

`pr 360 / 5` divides and prints answer in Print window

`setc red` changes drawing color to red

Tools

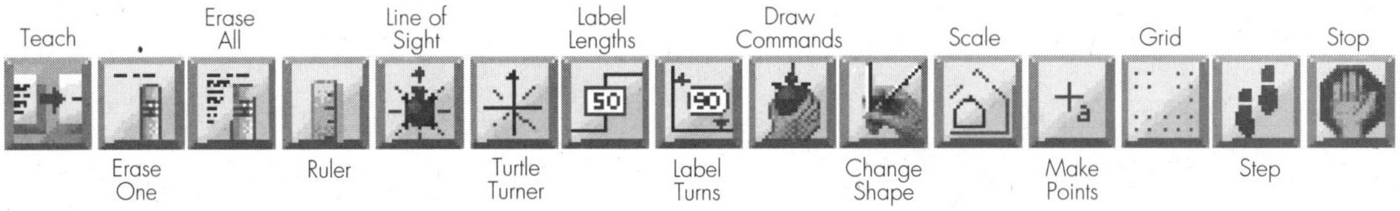

How to Get Help from *Geo-Logo*

- Choose a topic from the **Help** menu.

How to Open Saved Work

- Turn on the computer, open *Geo-Logo*.
- Choose **Open My Work**.
- Click the name of your work.
- Click **Open**.

How to Save Your Work

- Choose **Save My Work** from the **File** menu.
- First time, type a name like this: `DC+GW Rect 10/23`
- Click **Save**.

How to Finish

- Finish activity: Choose **Close My Work** from the **File** menu.
  STOP HERE if changing users.
- Finish *Geo-Logo*: Choose **Quit** from the **File** menu.
- Shut down and turn off the computer.

GUESS MY RULE CARDS (page 1 of 2)

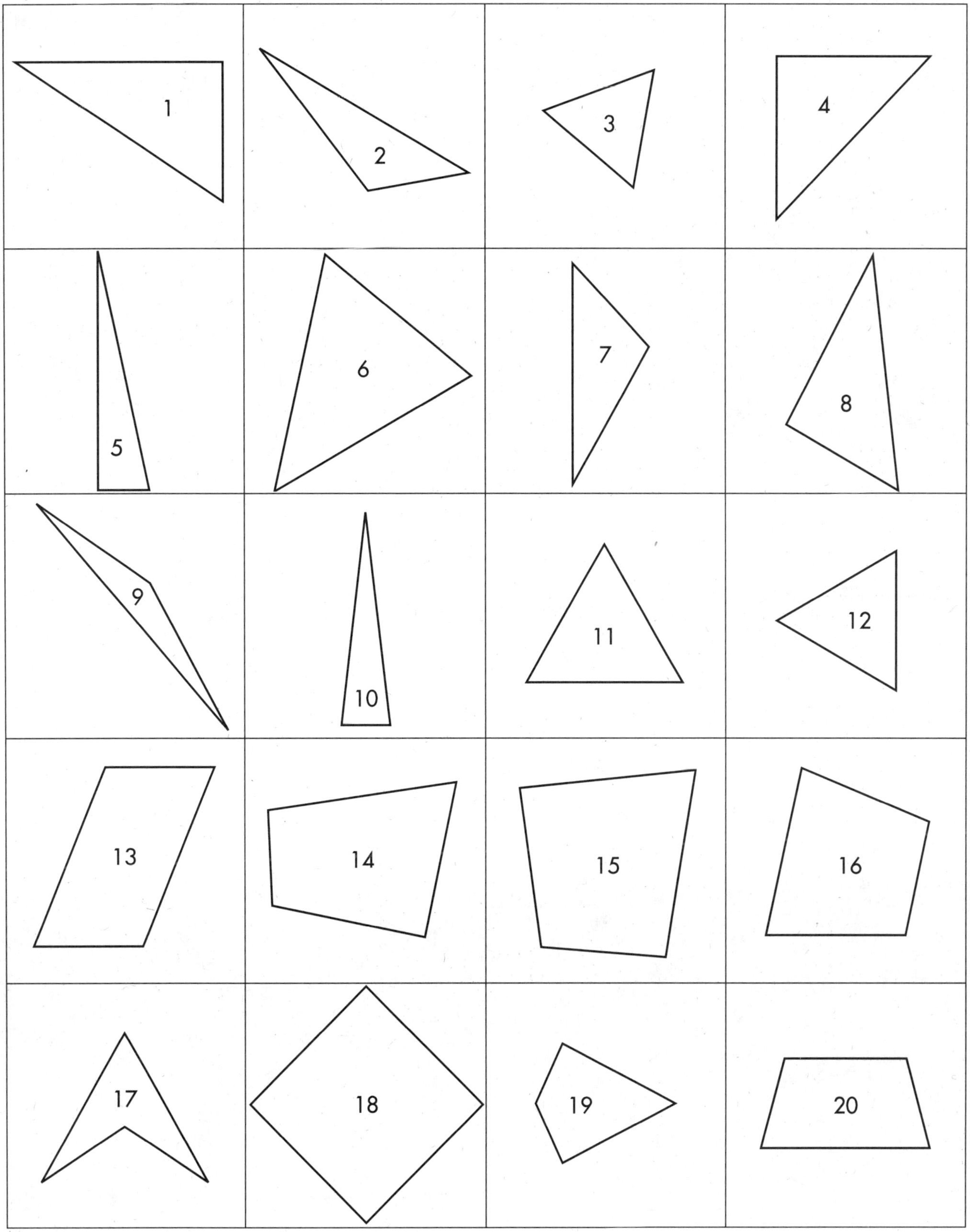

GUESS MY RULE CARDS (page 2 of 2)

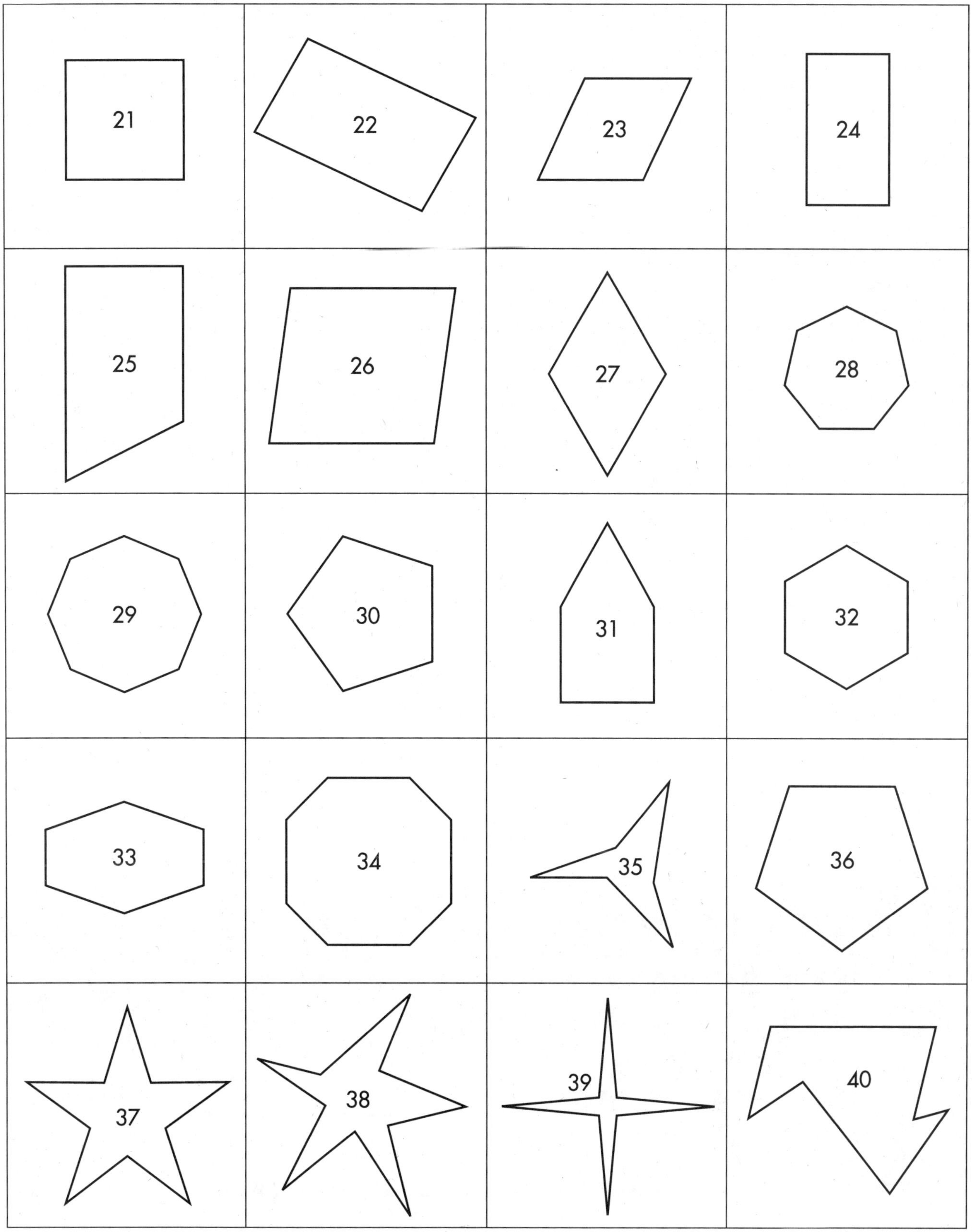

Name Date

Student Sheet 6

Is Every Three-Sided Polygon a Triangle?

Answer the following question, and draw sketches to illustrate your ideas.

Is every polygon with three sides a triangle? Why or why not?

To the Family

Is Every Three-Sided Polygon a Triangle?

Sessions 1–3

Math Content
Reasoning and communicating about geometric shapes

Materials
Student Sheet 6
Pencil

In class, students have been sorting polygons, carefully examining the characteristics of three-sided figures. For homework, students will answer this question: Are all three-sided polygons triangles? They will justify their reasoning with both words and pictures on Student Sheet 6.

Name Date

Is Every Square a Rectangle? Is Every Rectangle a Square?

Answer the following questions, and draw sketches to illustrate your ideas.

Is every square a rectangle? Why or why not?

Is every rectangle a square? Why or why not?

To the Family

Is Every Square a Rectangle? Is Every Rectangle a Square?

Sessions 1–3

Math Content
Reasoning and communicating about geometric shapes

Materials
Student Sheet 7
Pencil

For homework, your child will answer these questions: Can a square be a rectangle? Can a rectangle be a square? Your child will answer these questions using both words and pictures.

Name Date

How to Play Guess My Rule with Shapes

Materials: Deck of Guess My Rule cards

Two areas for grouping shapes according to whether or not they fit a rule—for example, a circle made of string or two different pieces of paper.

Players: 2

How to Play

1. The first player chooses a rule and gives a few examples, putting those shapes that fit the rule in one place (e.g., inside the circle) and those shapes that do not in the other place (e.g., outside the circle). The rule should focus on properties of geometric shapes, such as the shapes in the circle being all right triangles, all triangles with at least one right angle, or all quadrilaterals that are not squares.
2. The second player tries to guess the rule by placing a shape either inside or outside the circle, depending on whether the player thinks it fits the rule or not.
3. The first player says whether or not the placement is correct.
4. The second player uses this information to eliminate possibilities, devise new solutions, and revise earlier guesses of what the rule might be. Using this new information, the second player again tries to guess where a particular shape belongs.
5. Repeat steps 3 and 4. The second player can guess a rule if the player thinks he or she has found a solution. The first player says whether or not the rule is correct.
6. Play continues until the second player guesses the rule or there are no shapes left to place.

To the Family

Guess My Rule

Sessions 1–3

Math Content
Sorting and classifying triangles and quadrilaterals

Materials
Student Sheet 8
Guess My Rule Cards
Yarn, string, or blank paper

For homework, your child will ask up to four people at home to play a game called Guess My Rule. The complete directions for the game are on Student Sheet 8.

GUESS MY RULE CARDS (page 1 of 2)

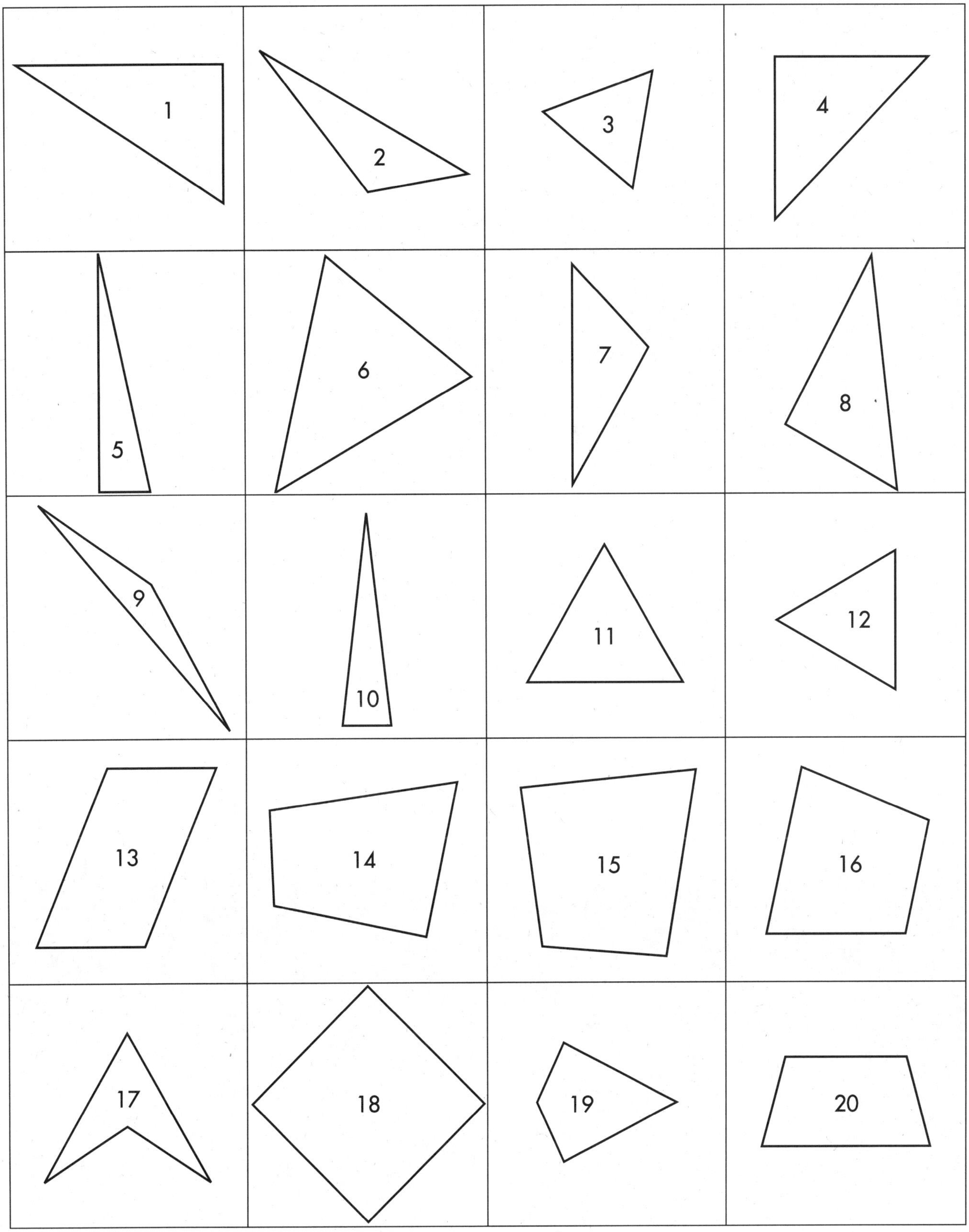

GUESS MY RULE CARDS (page 2 of 2)

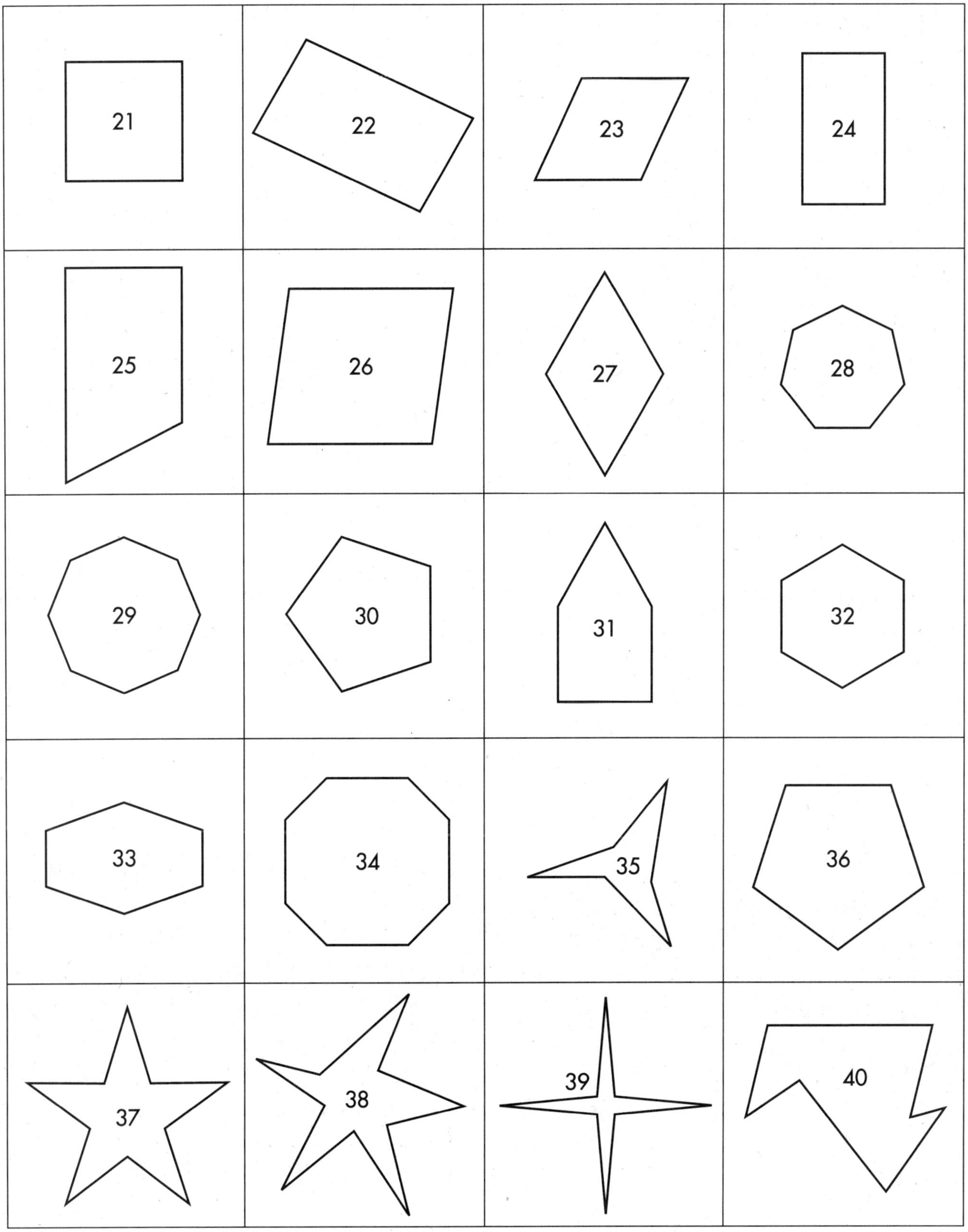

Name Date

Student Sheet 10

Can You Make These Quadrilaterals?

	Length of sides	Angles	Number of parallel sides	Name of shape	Setxy points that make this quadrilateral	Sketch of Power Polygons that make this quadrilateral
quad1	2 pairs of equal sides	4 right angles	2 pairs			
quad2	4 equal sides	0 right angles	2 pairs			
quad3	0 equal sides	4 right angles	your choice			
quad4	your choice	exactly 2 right angles	1 pair			
quad5	your choice	your choice	0 pairs			

Do you think any of these quadrilaterals are impossible?
If so, pick one and write about how you could prove it is impossible.

To the Family

Coordinate Grids and "Quad" or "Tri" Commands

Sessions 4–5

Math Content
Generating geometric figures from a description of their properties

Materials
Student Sheet 3
Student Sheets 9 and 10 (partially filled in)
Pencil

In class, students have been following a set of rules to produce a quadrilateral or triangle. They have been making these shapes with manipulatives as well as on the computer using *Geo-Logo.* For homework, your child will be referring to the recording sheet for this in-class activity and will be writing computer commands for any polygons not yet drawn on the computer.

Name Date

Student Sheet 3

Coordinate Grids

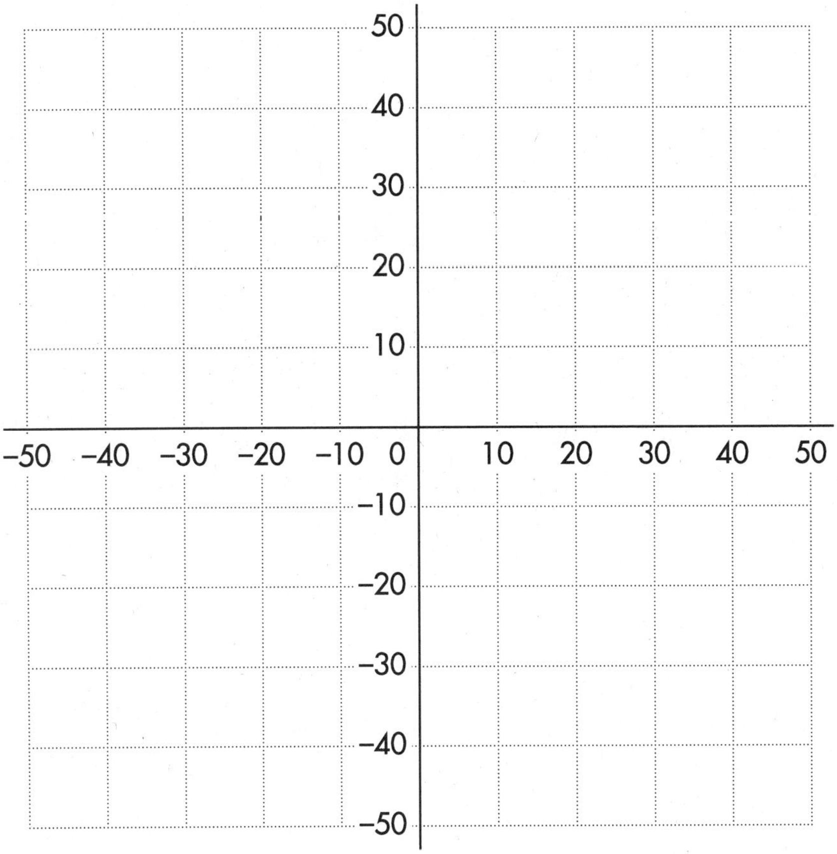

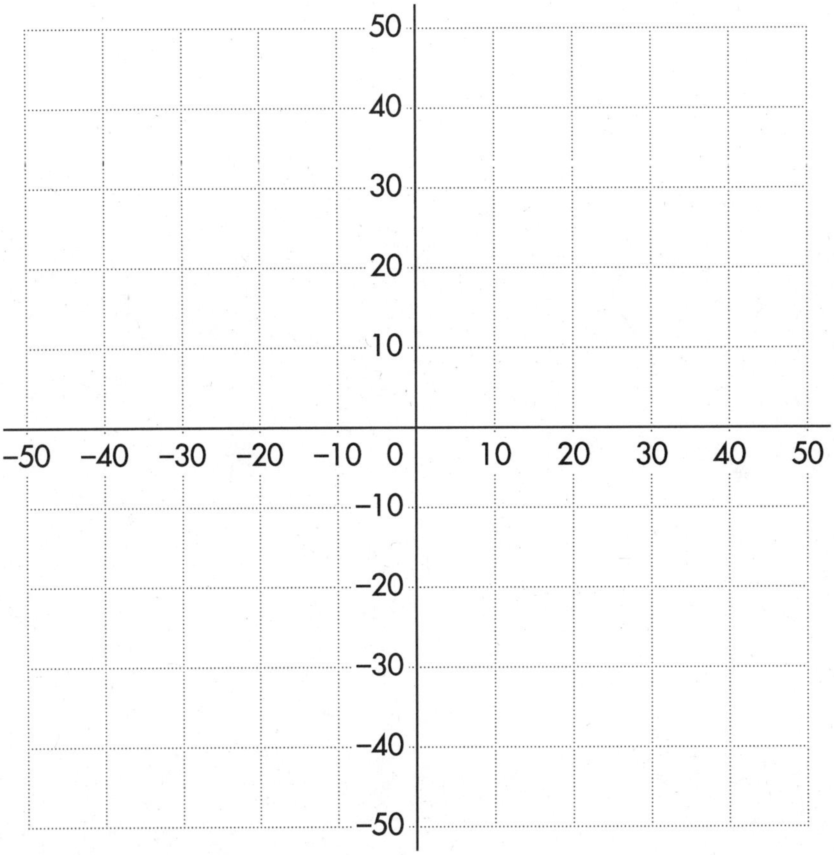

Name Date

Student Sheet 3

Coordinate Grids

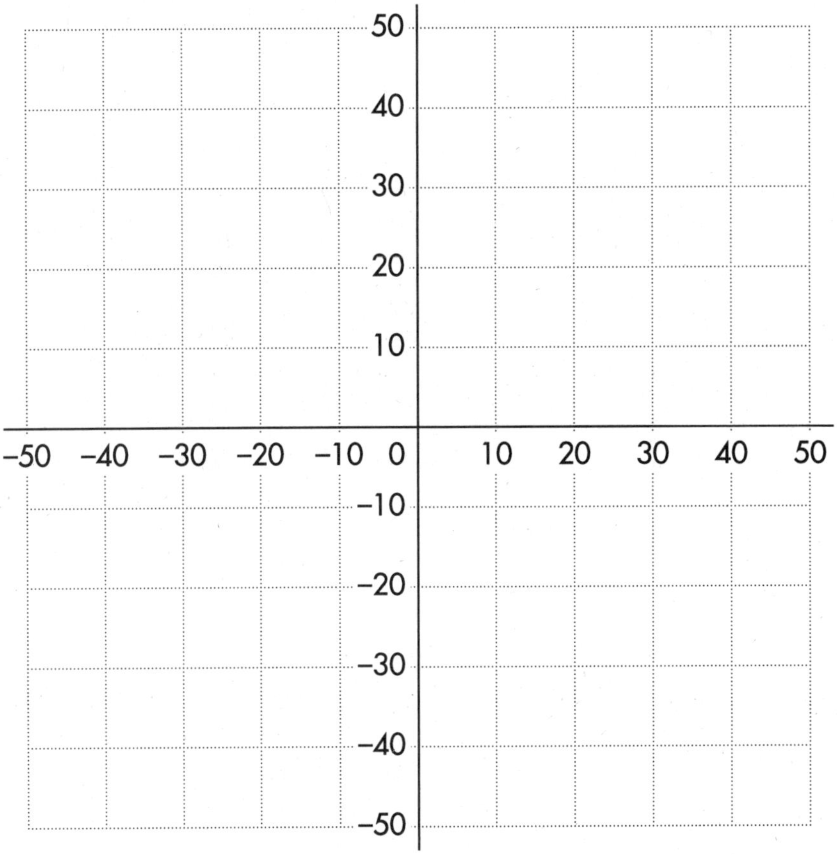

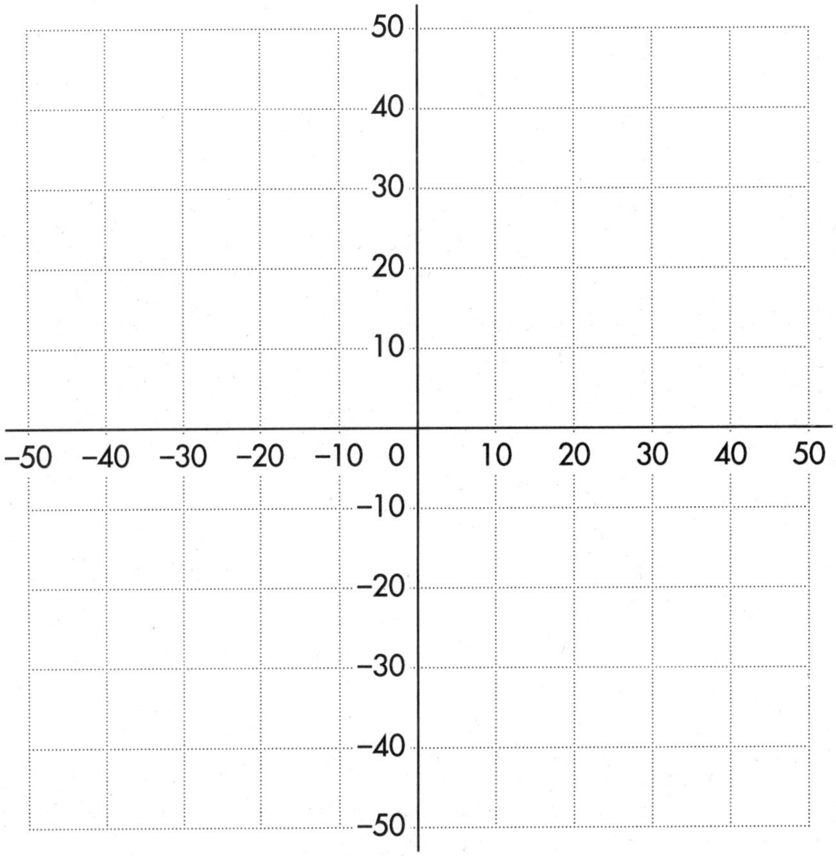

Name Date

Student Sheet 3

Coordinate Grids

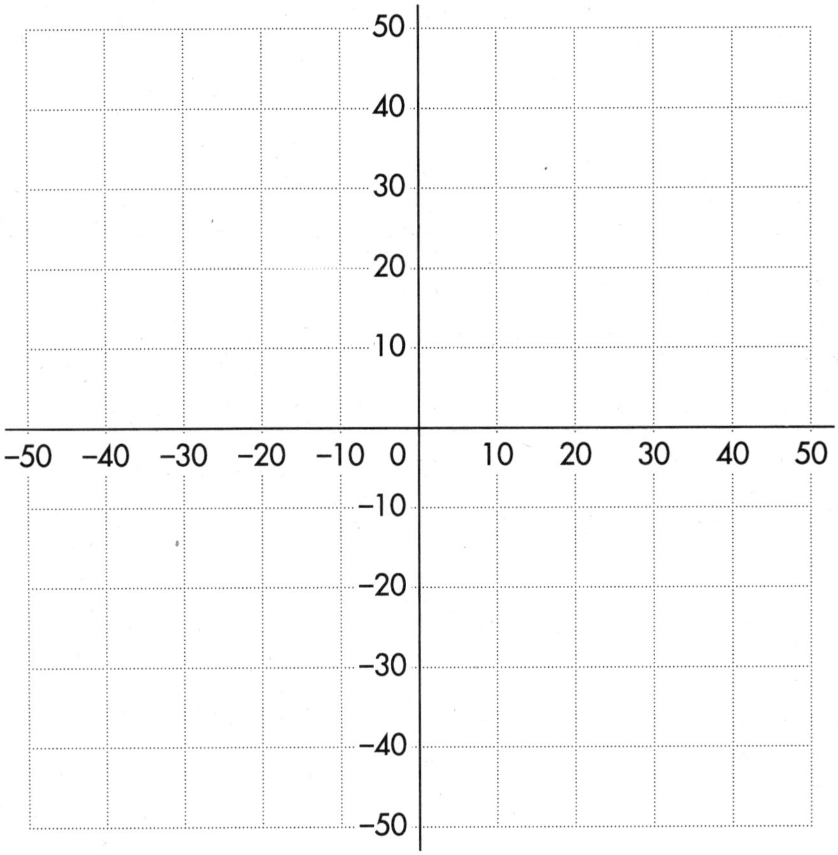

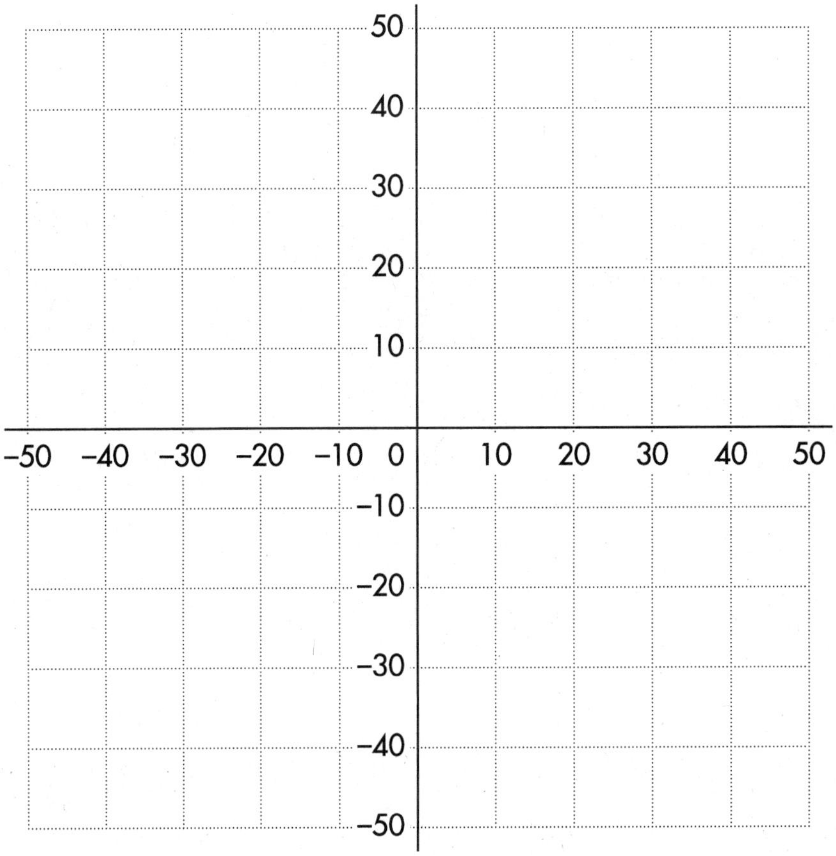

Name Date

Student Sheet 3

Coordinate Grids

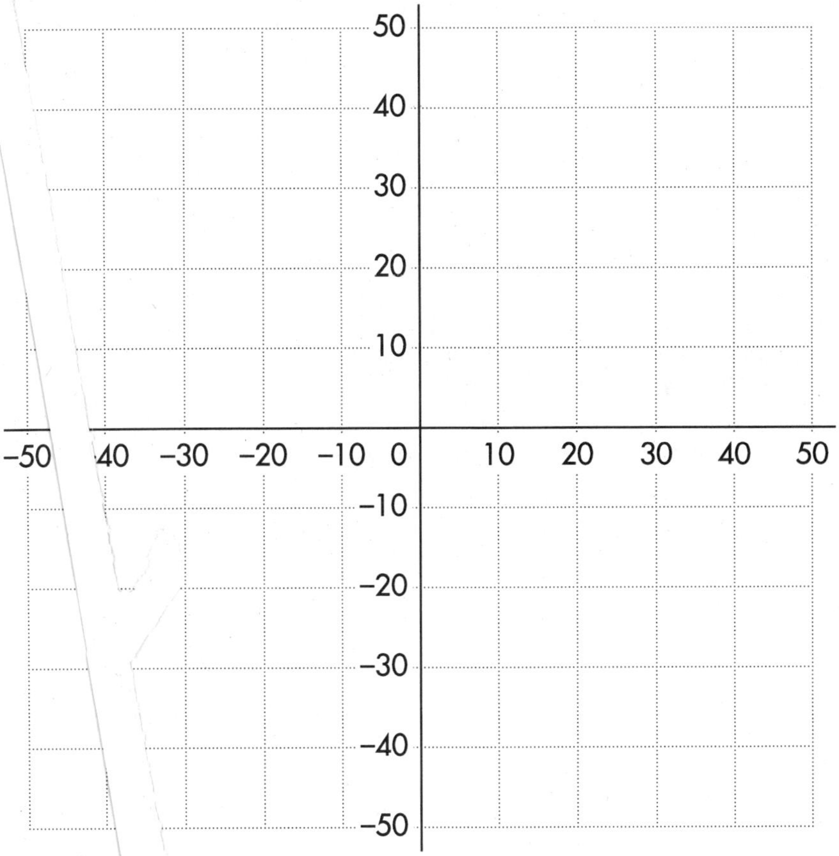

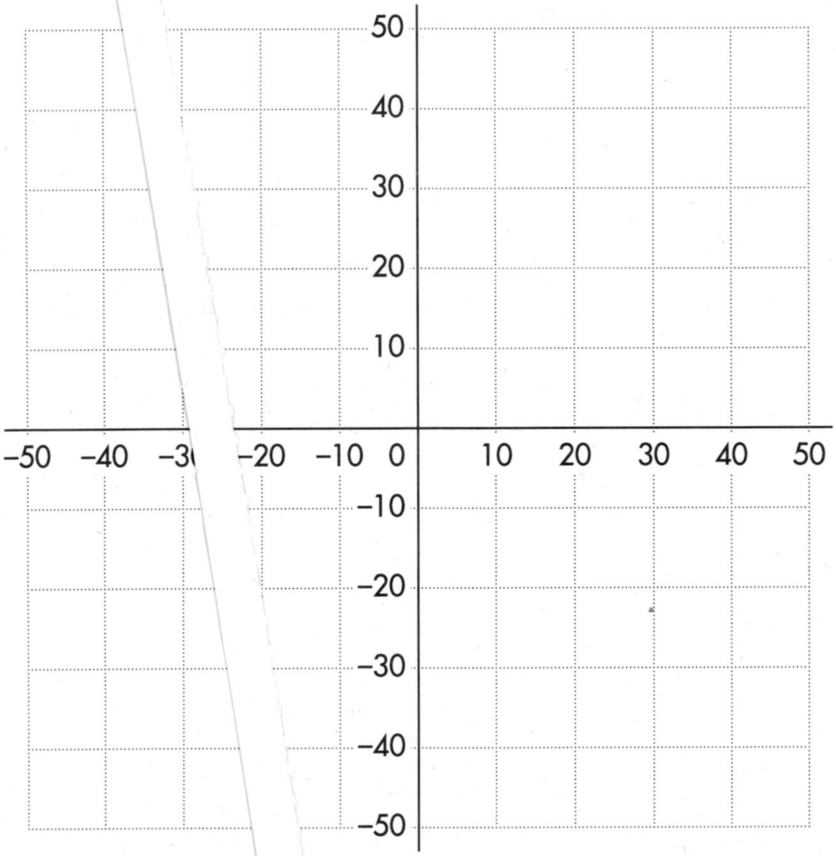

To the Family

Coordinate Grids and "Quad" or "Tri" Commands

Sessions 4–5

Math Content
Generating geometric figures from a description of their properties

Materials
Student Sheet 3
Student Sheets 9 and 10 (partially filled in)
Pencil

In class, students have been following a set of rules to produce a quadrilateral or triangle. They have been making these shapes with manipulatives as well as on the computer using *Geo-Logo*. For homework, your child will be referring to the recording sheet for this in-class activity and will be writing computer commands for any polygons not yet drawn on the computer.

Name Date

Coordinate Grids

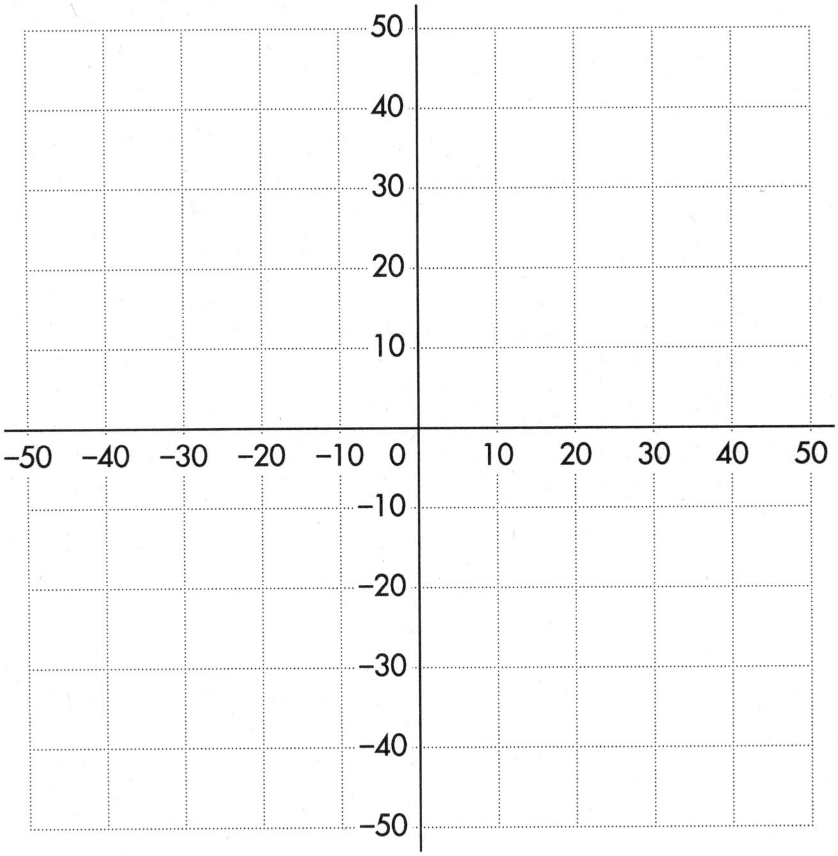

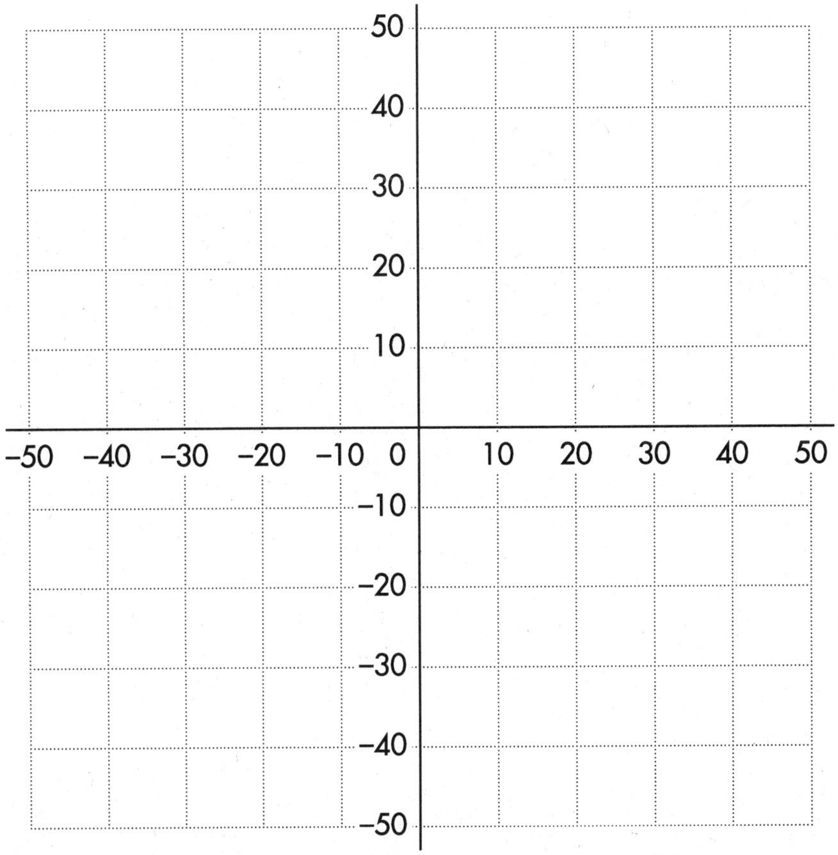

To the Family

Coordinate Grids and "Quad" or "Tri" Commands

Sessions 4–5

Math Content
Generating geometric figures from a description of their properties

Materials
Student Sheet 3
Student Sheets 9 and 10 (partially filled in)
Pencil

In class, students have been following a set of rules to produce a quadrilateral or triangle. They have been making these shapes with manipulatives as well as on the computer using *Geo-Logo.* For homework, your child will be referring to the recording sheet for this in-class activity and will be writing computer commands for any polygons not yet drawn on the computer.

Name Date

Student Sheet 11

Find the Fourth Vertex

These are the coordinates of three points:

(0, 10)

(30, 10)

(20, –30)

Find a fourth point so that the four points form the vertices of a parallelogram.

How would you do this?

How many different points could be the fourth vertex?

What are the coordinates of these points?

Write your answers below.

Show the different possible parallelograms in different colors on the grid.

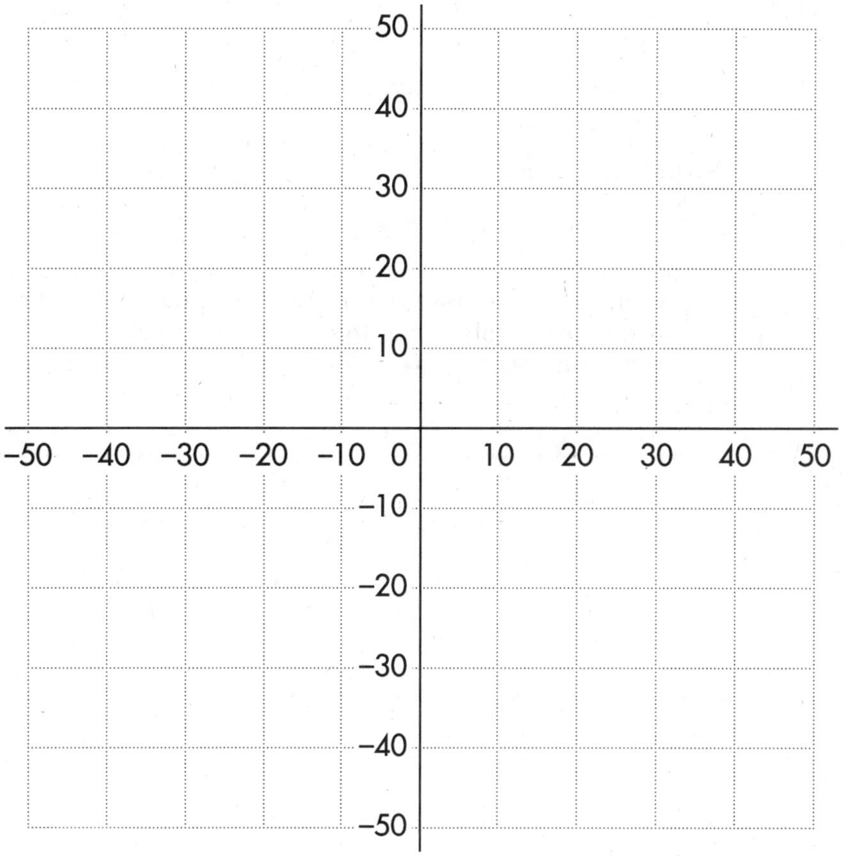

To the Family

Find the Fourth Vertex

Sessions 4–5

Math Content
Generating geometric figures from descriptions of properties

Materials
Student Sheet 11
Pencil

For homework, your child will be finding the fourth point for a quadrilateral, given the first three points on Student Sheet 11. We will be discussing these problems in tomorrow's math class, so you might want to remind your child to take the student sheet back to class.

Some Shapes Fit Many Categories

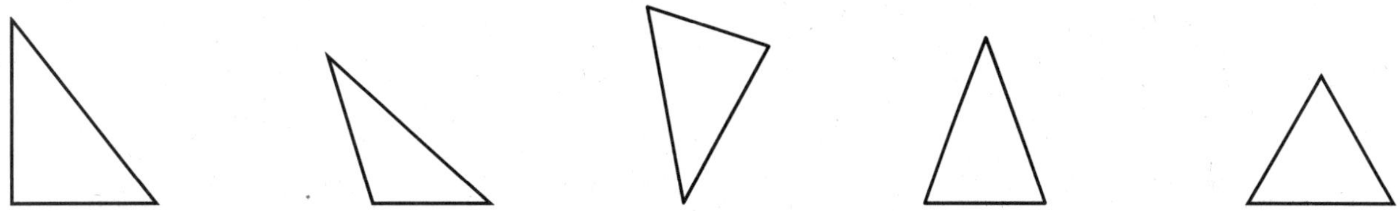

right triangle (1 right angle)

obtuse triangle (1 angle larger than 90°)

scalene triangle (no equal sides)

isosceles triangle (2 equal sides)

equilateral triangle (3 equal sides, 3 equal angles)

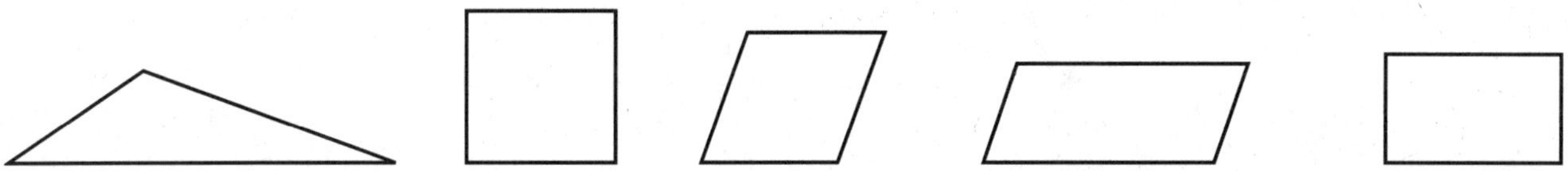

obtuse scalene triangle (1 angle larger than 90°, no equal sides)

square (4 equal sides, 4 right angles)

rhombus (4 equal sides)

parallelogram (opposite sides parallel)

rectangle (4 right angles)

1. A square is a kind of rhombus. How can this be?

2. Name all the shapes above that are parallelograms. How can they be parallelograms and have other names as well?

3. An equilateral triangle is isosceles. How can this be?

4. Some obtuse triangles are scalene. Some obtuse triangles are isosceles. Sketch one or two examples of each.

5. Obtuse triangles cannot be equilateral. Explain why this is true.

Name Date

Student Sheet 13

What Shape Does It Draw?

Write the letter of each procedure in the shape that it draws.
Then write the procedure for the shape that is left.

```
to A
fd 20
rt 120
fd 20
rt 60
fd 20
rt 120
fd 20
rt 60
end
```

```
to B
fd 20
rt 60
fd 20
rt 150
fd 35
rt 150
end
```

```
to C
fd 20
rt 120
fd 20
rt 120
fd 20
rt 120
end
```

```
to D
fd 20
rt 90
fd 20
rt 90
fd 20
rt 90
fd 20
rt 90
end
```

```
to E
```

1. 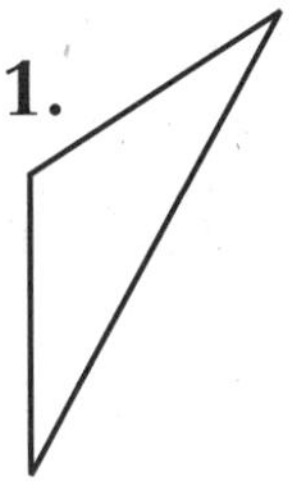

2. 

3. 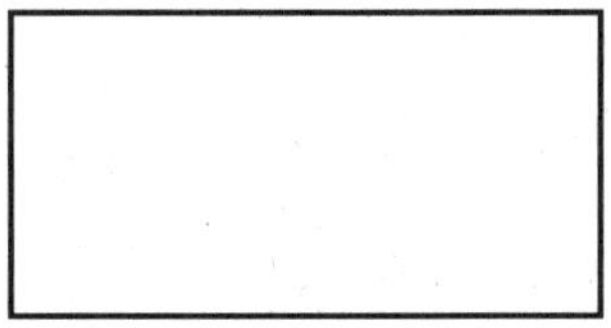

4. 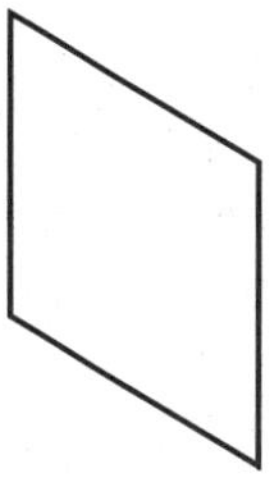

5. 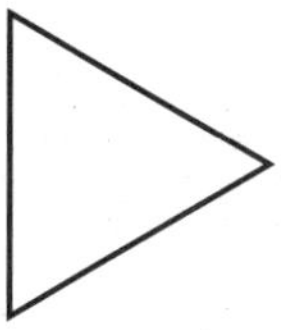

Challenge 1
Write a procedure to draw this shape.

Challenge 2
Pretend you are the turtle.
Draw the shape that this procedure would draw.
Use a separate sheet of paper.

```
to drawme
lt 90
fd 5
rt 90
fd 10
lt 90
fd 15
rt 125
fd 35
rt 110
fd 35
rt 125
fd 15
lt 90
fd 10
rt 90
fd 5
end
```

To the Family

What Shape Does It Draw?

Sessions 6–7

Math Content

Seeing relationships between turns and angles
Visualizing geometric figures from a description of computer commands

Materials

Student Sheet 13
Pencil

For homework, your child will be figuring out which polygon a set of computer commands would draw. In class, students have been using similar commands to produce polygons to learn more about geometric properties. Your child might want to try the two challenges as well. The first challenge asks the student to write a procedure to draw a particular shape. The second asks the student to draw the shape a set of computer commands would draw.

Name Date

Student Sheet 14

Angles in the Power Polygons (page 1 of 2)

Label each angle with its size. Explain how you figured out the size of each angle.

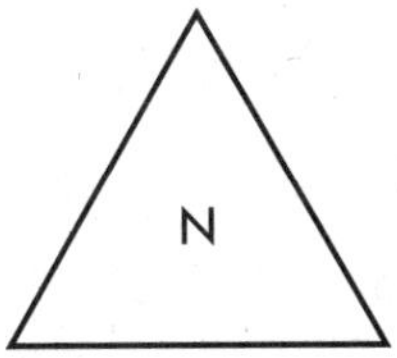

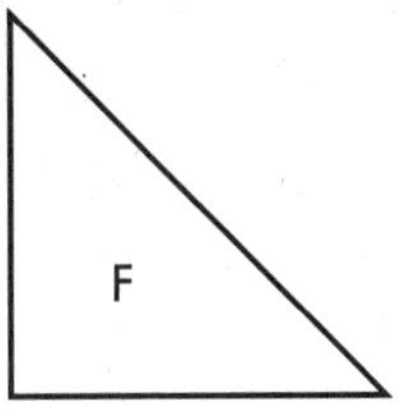

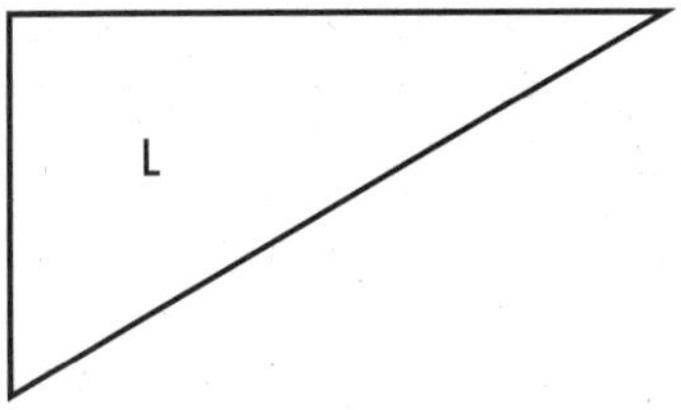

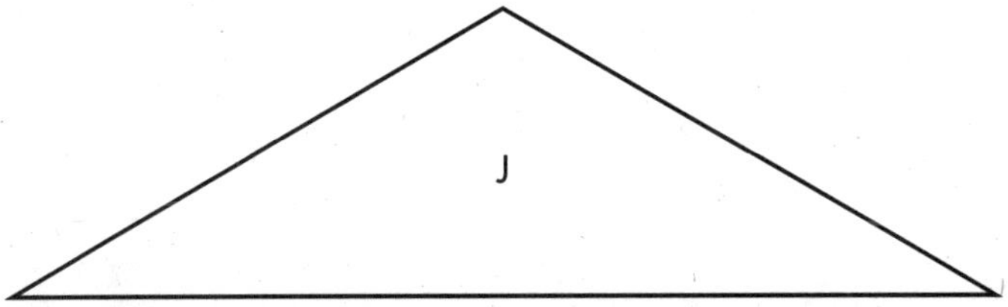

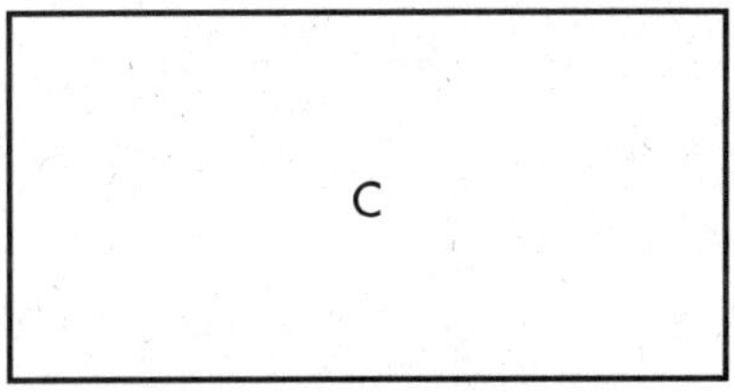

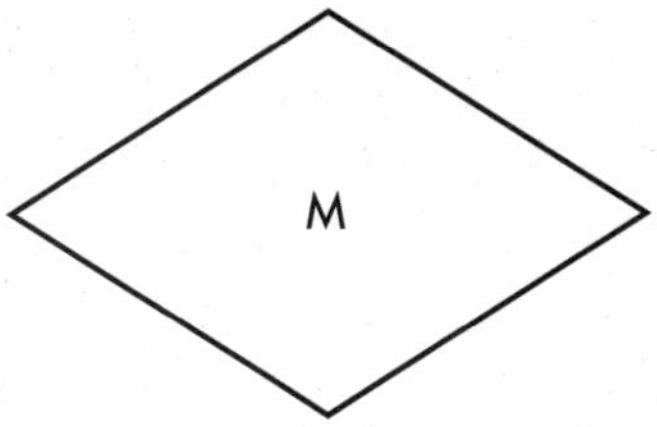

Name Date

Angles in the Power Polygons (page 2 of 2)

Label each angle with its size. Explain how you figured out the size of each angle.

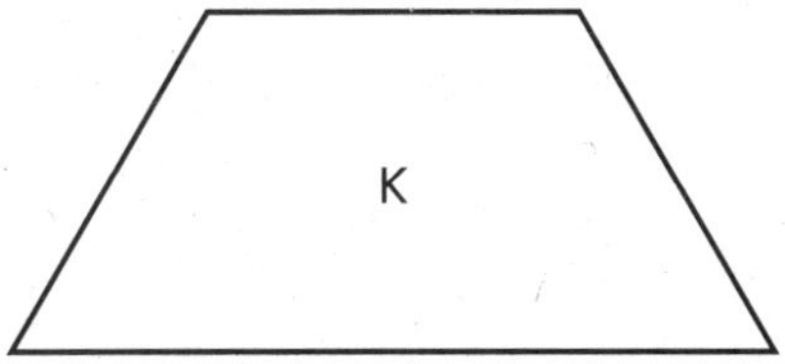

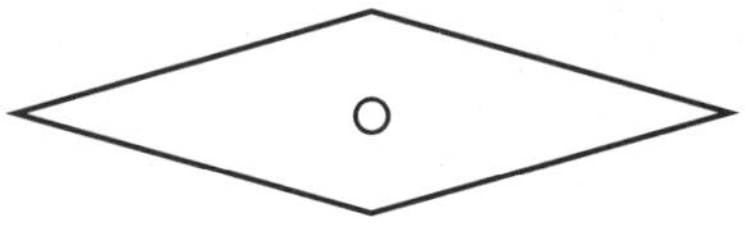

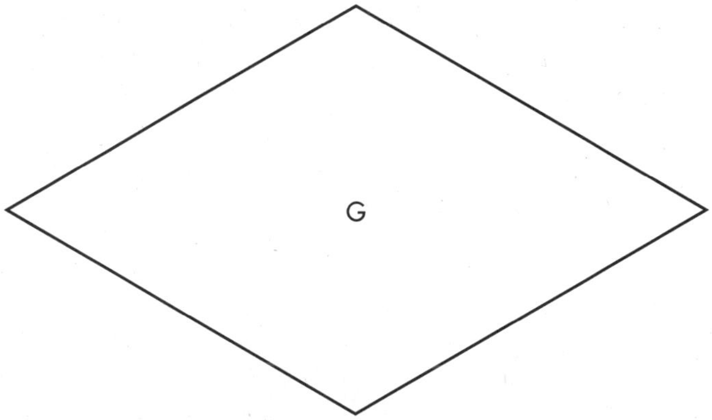

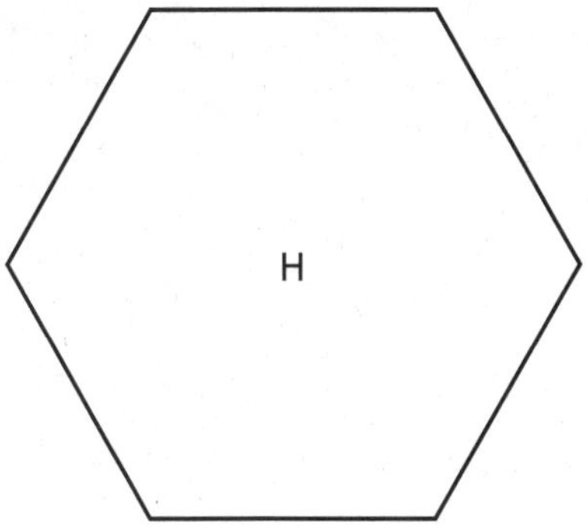

Name Date

Student Sheet 16

Angles and Turns

Imagine the turtle walks straight up the left side of each triangle. What **turn** does it make to head down the next side? What other turns will it need to make as it walks around the shape?

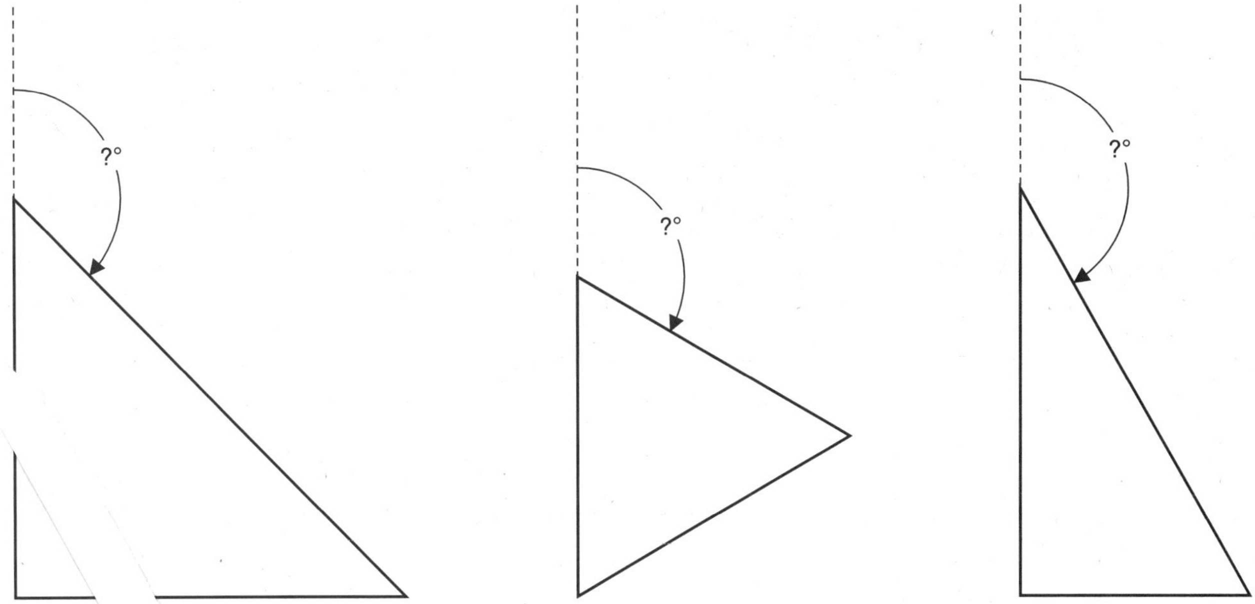

Figure the number of degrees in the marked **angles** and write the n. What sizes are the other angles in the triangles?

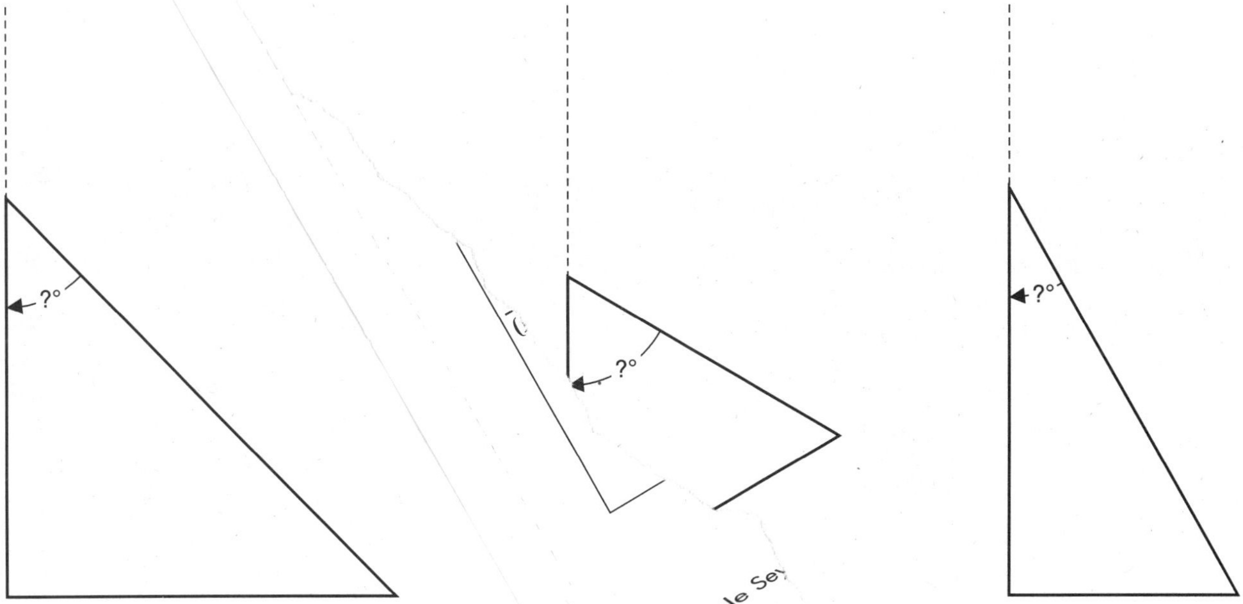

How are the angle size and the ated?

Name Date

Student Sheet 17

What Do You Know About 45° and 60° Angles?

Write about the two questions below. Include the following in your answers.

1. where you see 45° and 60° angles
2. the names of some polygons containing these angles
3. how 45° and 60° angles compare with other angles
4. how many of each angle you need to make a full circle or a straight line

What do you know about 45° angles?

____

____

____

____

____

What do you know about 60° angles?

____

____

____

____

____

To the Family

What Do You Know About 45° and 60° Angles?

Session 9

Math Content

Drawing conclusions from data gathered about angles

Materials

Student Sheet 17
Pencil

In class these past weeks, students have had a lot of experience identifying, determining, and creating different angles. For homework, your child will continue to write what he or she knows about 45° and 60° angles on Student Sheet 17. Some things your child might write about include the following: Where do we see a 60° angle? a 45° angle? What sketches can you draw of shapes with these angles? How do these angles compare with other angles, such as 90° angles or 180° angles? How many of each angle do you need to make a full circle?

Name Date

Student Sheet 18

Total Turns and Angles (page 1 of 2)

Complete the chart below, working on or off the computer. You may use drawings or Power Polygons to help.

Polygon	Number of sides, turns, angles	Length of sides (turtle steps)	Size of each turn (degrees)	Sum of turns	Size of each angle (degrees)	Sum of angles
equilateral triangle	3					
square	4					
regular pentagon	5					
regular hexagon	6					
regular heptagon (a challenge!)	7					
regular octagon	8					
regular nonagon	9					
regular decagon	10					

When you have finished the chart, write about any patterns you notice.

To the Family

Total Turns and Angles

Sessions 1–2

Math Content

Finding patterns for turns, angles, and the sums of turns and angles for regular polygons

Materials

Student Sheet 18
Turtle Turner
Pencil

In class, students have been working on completing this sheet by filling in the first three columns for each figure and then calculating the size of each turn in degrees, the sum of turns, the size of each angle in degrees, and the sum of all the angles inside the polygon. For homework, your child will continue filling in this sheet and then look for patterns that will help her or him find the values for a seven-sided polygon. Those who finish the chart should extend it and figure the values for polygons with 15 and 20 sides. Your child should record this work on the back of Student Sheet 18. Your child may use the Turtle Turner while doing this assignment.

Name Date

Total Turns and Angles (page 2 of 2)

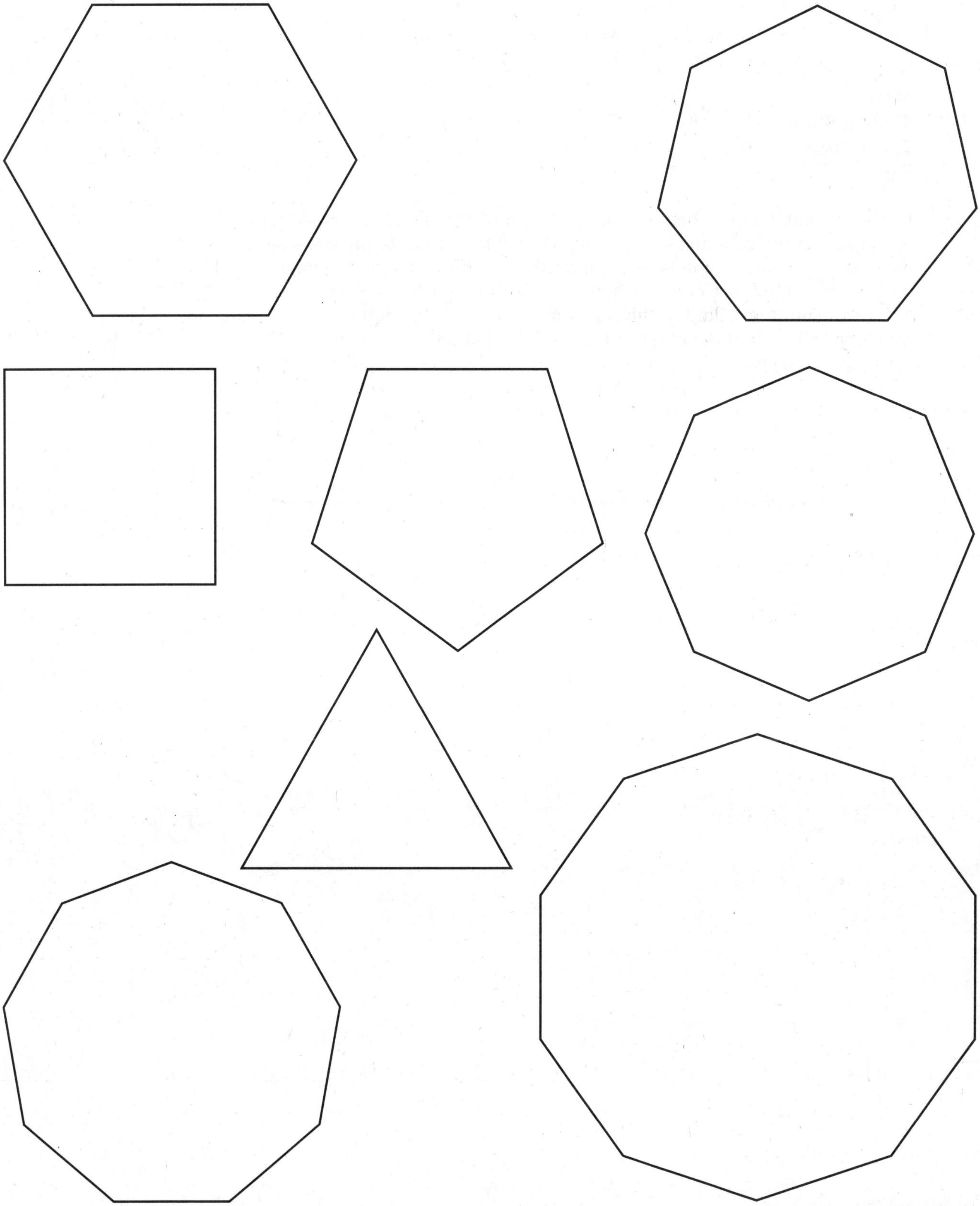

To the Family

Total Turns and Angles

Sessions 1–2

Math Content

Finding patterns for turns, angles, and the sums of turns and angles for regular polygons

Materials

Student Sheet 18
Turtle Turner
Pencil

In class, students have been working on completing this sheet by filling in the first three columns for each figure and then calculating the size of each turn in degrees, the sum of turns, the size of each angle in degrees, and the sum of all the angles inside the polygon. For homework, your child will continue filling in this sheet and then look for patterns that will help her or him find the values for a seven-sided polygon. Those who finish the chart should extend it and figure the values for polygons with 15 and 20 sides. Your child should record this work on the back of Student Sheet 18. Your child may use the Turtle Turner while doing this assignment.

Name Date

Student Sheet 19

Which Are Regular Polygons?

Below are scale drawings of shapes made with Power Polygons. Tell whether each shape is a regular polygon. Explain in writing how you know.

1. Is this a regular polygon? ________________ How do you know?

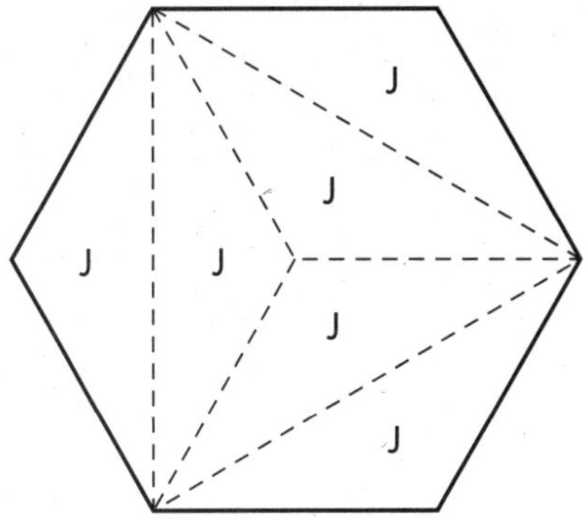

2. Is this a regular polygon? ________________ How do you know?

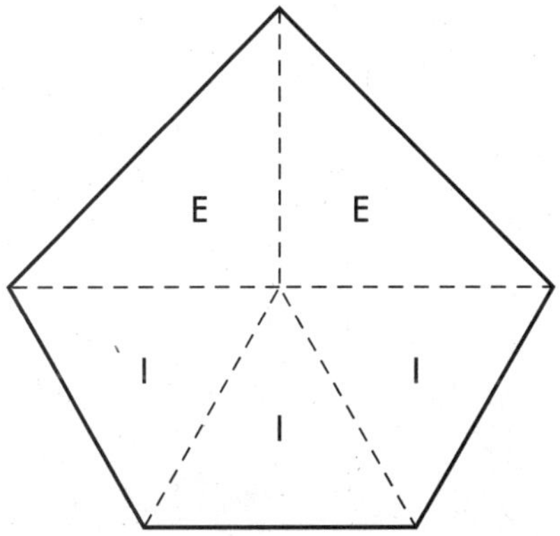

3. Is this a regular polygon? ________________ How do you know?

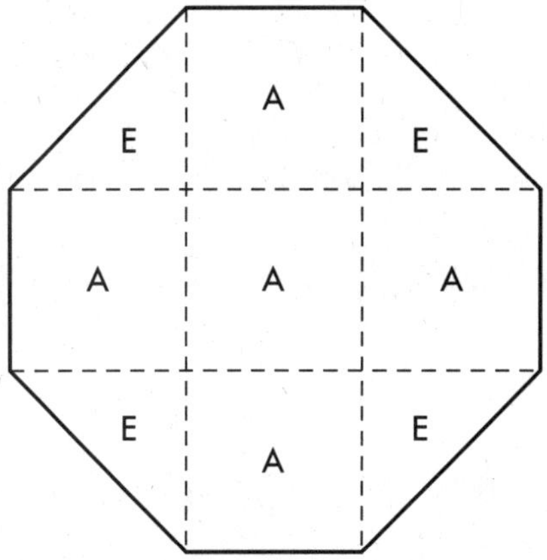

Name Date

Student Sheet 20

Polygons That Are Not Regular

Circle the group or groups you are to work with.

Group A: triangles and decagons
Group B: quadrilaterals and heptagons
Group C: pentagons and octagons
Group D: hexagons and nonagons

Draw at least two examples, with different-sized angles, of the nonregular polygons for your group(s). Measure the angles of each polygon with the Turtle Turner, and add them to find the sum.

To the Family

Polygons That Are Not Regular

Session 3

Math Content
Finding patterns in measures of nonregular polygons

Materials
Student Sheet 20
Turtle Turner
Pencil

Recently, your child explored the relationship between the sum of the angles and the number of sides in a polygon. The homework assignment is to see if these patterns also hold for polygons that are not regular. Your child may use the Turtle Turner to help with this assignment. Your child will be calculating the total sum of angles in each of two examples from the group of nonregular polygons assigned for homework.

Name Date

Student Sheet 21

Building Similar Shapes

Use Power Polygons. Build similar figures for each shape. Keep track of how many of each shape it takes to build the second larger shape, the third larger shape, and the fourth larger shape. **Predict** how many pieces it will take to build the tenth larger shape.

	Number of pieces in similar (larger) shapes					
Shape	1st	2nd	3rd	4th	5th	10th
B (square)						
C (rectangle)						
H (hexagon)						
J (obtuse isosceles triangle)						
K (trapezoid)						
M (rhombus)						
N (equilateral triangle)						
0 (thin rhombus)						

In the space below, show how you built the second trapezoid or hexagon by tracing around the shapes. On the back of this sheet, show how you built the third trapezoid or hexagon.

Name Date

Student Sheet 22

Length of Sides Versus Area

Answer the following questions. Use sketches to help explain your answers.

1. When we double the length of the sides of a polygon, the area is 4 times as large. Why? Why not 2 times as large?

2. When we triple the length of the sides of a polygon, the area is 9 times as large. Why? Why not 3 times as large?

To the Family

Length of Sides Versus Area

Session 4

Math Content

Expressing the relationship between side lengths and area in similar polygons

Materials

Student Sheet 22
Pencil

In class, students have been investigating how area increases in relationship to the number of sides added to a figure. For homework, your child will be answering questions related to this exploration.

Name _______________ Date _______________

Student Sheet 23

Similar Rectangles

Choose the *Geo-Logo* activity Similar Rectangles. The turtle draws the original rectangle in the Drawing window.

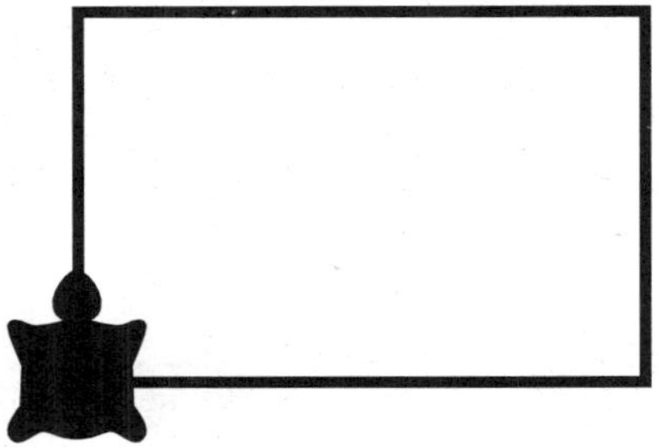

Write procedures to draw rectangles that are similar to the original rectangle. To check your procedures, use the Scale tool. See if the new rectangle stretches or shrinks to have exactly the same numbers as the original rectangle.

Original rectangle	Similar rectangle 1		Similar rectangle 2		Similar rectangle 3		Similar rectangle 4	
	Predict ☐	Corrected	Predict ☐	Corrected	Predict ☐	Corrected	Predict ☐	Corrected
fd 10	fd 20		fd 30		fd 16		fd 24	
rt 90	rt		rt		rt		rt	
fd 15	fd		fd		fd		fd	
rt 90	rt		rt		rt		rt	
fd 10	fd		fd		fd		fd	
rt 90	rt		rt		rt		rt	
fd 15	fd		fd		fd		fd	
rt 90	rt		rt		rt		rt	

Name ____________________ Date ____________

Student Sheet 24

Similar Houses

Choose the *Geo-Logo* activity Similar Houses. The turtle draws the original house in the Drawing window.

Write procedures to draw houses that are similar to the original house. Use the Scale tool to check your work.

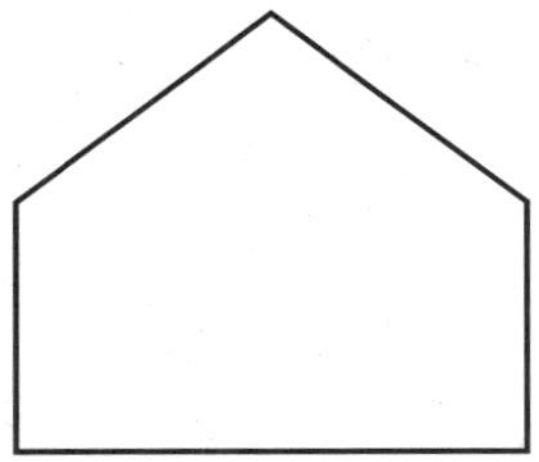

Original house	Double		Triple		Half		Challenge	
	Predict ☐	Corrected	Predict ☐	Corrected	Predict ☐	Corrected	Predict ☐	Corrected
fd 8	fd 16		fd 24		fd 4		fd 20	
rt 53.1	rt		rt		rt		rt	
fd 10	fd		fd		fd		fd	
rt 73.8	rt		rt		rt		rt	
fd 10	fd		fd		fd		fd	
rt 53.1	rt		rt		rt		rt	
fd 8	fd		fd		fd		fd	
rt 90	rt		rt		rt		rt	
fd 16	fd		fd		fd		fd	
rt 90	rt		rt		rt		rt	

On the back of this sheet, explain how you found the commands for the triple-size house.

Name Date

Student Sheet 25

Drawing More Similar Rectangles

On pieces of one-centimeter graph paper, draw a rectangle and then draw another that is similar to it.

Challenge someone at home to draw yet another rectangle that is similar to the first two. Or provide one side of the similar rectangle, and challenge someone to draw the rest, making it similar to the original.

Take turns challenging each other. Experiment with both wide and narrow rectangles, and make a few that are similar to each.

To the Family

Drawing More Similar Rectangles

Sessions 5–6

Math Content

Exploring the relationship between side lengths and areas of similar shapes

Materials

Student Sheet 25
2–3 sheets of one-centimeter graph paper
Pencil

For homework, your child will draw a rectangle on graph paper and then draw another one that is "similar" to it, as you might do in drawing a scale drawing. After your child has drawn these rectangles, he or she will challenge someone at home to draw yet another rectangle that is similar to the first two. Your child may also draw a side of a third rectangle and ask someone at home to make it similar to the first two using this side as a start. Your child and the person being challenged should take turns challenging each other to draw similar shapes by drawing several similar rectangles, including wide and narrow rectangles.

ONE-CENTIMETER GRAPH PAPER

ONE-CENTIMETER GRAPH PAPER

ONE-CENTIMETER GRAPH PAPER

Name Date

How to Play Close to 0

Materials

- One deck of Numeral Cards
- Close to 0 Score Sheet for each player

Players: 1, 2, or 3

How to Play

1. Deal out eight Numeral Cards to each player.
2. Use any six cards to make two numbers. For example, a 6, a 5, and a 2 could make 652, 625, 526, 562, 256, or 265. Wild Cards can be used as any numeral. Try to make two numbers that, when subtracted, give you a difference that is close to 0.
3. Write these numbers and their difference on the Close to 0 Score Sheet. For example: 652 – 647 = 5. The difference is your score.
4. Put the cards you used in a discard pile. Keep the two cards you didn't use for the next round.
5. For the next round, deal six new cards to each player. Make two more numbers with a difference close to 0. When you run out of cards, mix up the discard pile and use them again.
6. After five rounds, total your scores. Lowest score wins.

Variation

Deal out ten Numeral Cards to each player. Each player uses eight cards to make two numbers that, when subtracted, give a total close to 0.

Name ____________________ Date ____________________

Close to 0 Score Sheet

Game 1 — Score

Round 1: ___ ___ ___ – ___ ___ ___ = ________ ________

Round 2: ___ ___ ___ – ___ ___ ___ = ________ ________

Round 3: ___ ___ ___ – ___ ___ ___ = ________ ________

Round 4: ___ ___ ___ – ___ ___ ___ = ________ ________

Round 5: ___ ___ ___ – ___ ___ ___ = ________ ________

TOTAL SCORE ________

Game 2 — Score

Round 1: ___ ___ ___ – ___ ___ ___ = ________ ________

Round 2: ___ ___ ___ – ___ ___ ___ = ________ ________

Round 3: ___ ___ ___ – ___ ___ ___ = ________ ________

Round 4: ___ ___ ___ – ___ ___ ___ = ________ ________

Round 5: ___ ___ ___ – ___ ___ ___ = ________ ________

TOTAL SCORE ________

Name ______________________________ Date ______________

Close to 0 Score Sheet

Game 1		Score
Round 1:	___ ___ ___ − ___ ___ ___ = ________	________
Round 2:	___ ___ ___ − ___ ___ ___ = ________	________
Round 3:	___ ___ ___ − ___ ___ ___ = ________	________
Round 4:	___ ___ ___ − ___ ___ ___ = ________	________
Round 5:	___ ___ ___ − ___ ___ ___ = ________	________
	TOTAL SCORE	________

Game 2		Score
Round 1:	___ ___ ___ − ___ ___ ___ = ________	________
Round 2:	___ ___ ___ − ___ ___ ___ = ________	________
Round 3:	___ ___ ___ − ___ ___ ___ = ________	________
Round 4:	___ ___ ___ − ___ ___ ___ = ________	________
Round 5:	___ ___ ___ − ___ ___ ___ = ________	________
	TOTAL SCORE	________

Name ____________________ Date ____________________

Close to 0 Score Sheet

Game 1	Score
Round 1: ___ ___ ___ – ___ ___ ___ = __________	__________
Round 2: ___ ___ ___ – ___ ___ ___ = __________	__________
Round 3: ___ ___ ___ – ___ ___ ___ = __________	__________
Round 4: ___ ___ ___ – ___ ___ ___ = __________	__________
Round 5: ___ ___ ___ – ___ ___ ___ = __________	__________
TOTAL SCORE	__________

Game 2	Score
Round 1: ___ ___ ___ – ___ ___ ___ = __________	__________
Round 2: ___ ___ ___ – ___ ___ ___ = __________	__________
Round 3: ___ ___ ___ – ___ ___ ___ = __________	__________
Round 4: ___ ___ ___ – ___ ___ ___ = __________	__________
Round 5: ___ ___ ___ – ___ ___ ___ = __________	__________
TOTAL SCORE	__________

Name ______________________________ Date ______________

Close to 0 Score Sheet

Game 1 — Score

Round 1: ___ ___ ___ – ___ ___ ___ = __________ __________

Round 2: ___ ___ ___ – ___ ___ ___ = __________ __________

Round 3: ___ ___ ___ – ___ ___ ___ = __________ __________

Round 4: ___ ___ ___ – ___ ___ ___ = __________ __________

Round 5: ___ ___ ___ – ___ ___ ___ = __________ __________

TOTAL SCORE __________

Game 2 — Score

Round 1: ___ ___ ___ – ___ ___ ___ = __________ __________

Round 2: ___ ___ ___ – ___ ___ ___ = __________ __________

Round 3: ___ ___ ___ – ___ ___ ___ = __________ __________

Round 4: ___ ___ ___ – ___ ___ ___ = __________ __________

Round 5: ___ ___ ___ – ___ ___ ___ = __________ __________

TOTAL SCORE __________

Name ______________________________ Date ______________________________

Close to 0 Score Sheet

Game 1				Score
Round 1:	___ ___ ___ – ___ ___ ___	=	__________	__________
Round 2:	___ ___ ___ – ___ ___ ___	=	__________	__________
Round 3:	___ ___ ___ – ___ ___ ___	=	__________	__________
Round 4:	___ ___ ___ – ___ ___ ___	=	__________	__________
Round 5:	___ ___ ___ – ___ ___ ___	=	__________	__________
			TOTAL SCORE	__________

Game 2				Score
Round 1:	___ ___ ___ – ___ ___ ___	=	__________	__________
Round 2:	___ ___ ___ – ___ ___ ___	=	__________	__________
Round 3:	___ ___ ___ – ___ ___ ___	=	__________	__________
Round 4:	___ ___ ___ – ___ ___ ___	=	__________	__________
Round 5:	___ ___ ___ – ___ ___ ___	=	__________	__________
			TOTAL SCORE	__________

Name ______________________________ Date ______________

Close to 0 Score Sheet

Game 1		Score
Round 1:	___ ___ ___ – ___ ___ ___ = ________	________
Round 2:	___ ___ ___ – ___ ___ ___ = ________	________
Round 3:	___ ___ ___ – ___ ___ ___ = ________	________
Round 4:	___ ___ ___ – ___ ___ ___ = ________	________
Round 5:	___ ___ ___ – ___ ___ ___ = ________	________
	TOTAL SCORE	________

Game 2		Score
Round 1:	___ ___ ___ – ___ ___ ___ = ________	________
Round 2:	___ ___ ___ – ___ ___ ___ = ________	________
Round 3:	___ ___ ___ – ___ ___ ___ = ________	________
Round 4:	___ ___ ___ – ___ ___ ___ = ________	________
Round 5:	___ ___ ___ – ___ ___ ___ = ________	________
	TOTAL SCORE	________

0	0	1	1
0	0	1	1
2	2	3	3
2	2	3	3

4	4	5	5
4	4	5	5
6	6	7	7
6	6	7	7

8	8	9	9
8	8	9	9
WILD CARD	WILD CARD		
WILD CARD	WILD CARD		

Name Date

Practice Page A

Solve this problem in two different ways, and write about how you solved it:

375 – 268 =

Here is the first way I solved it:

Here is the second way I solved it:

Name Date

Practice Page B

Solve this problem in two different ways, and write about how you solved it:

540 + 623 =

Here is the first way I solved it:

Here is the second way I solved it:

300 CHART

1	2	3	4	5	6	7	8	9	10
11	12	13	14	15	16	17	18	19	20
21	22	23	24	25	26	27	28	29	30
31	32	33	34	35	36	37	38	39	40
41	42	43	44	45	46	47	48	49	50
51	52	53	54	55	56	57	58	59	60
61	62	63	64	65	66	67	68	69	70
71	72	73	74	75	76	77	78	79	80
81	82	83	84	85	86	87	88	89	90
91	92	93	94	95	96	97	98	99	100
101	102	103	104	105	106	107	108	109	110
111	112	113	114	115	116	117	118	119	120
121	122	123	124	125	126	127	128	129	130
131	132	133	134	135	136	137	138	139	140
141	142	143	144	145	146	147	148	149	150
151	152	153	154	155	156	157	158	159	160
161	162	163	164	165	166	167	168	169	170
171	172	173	174	175	176	177	178	179	180
181	182	183	184	185	186	187	188	189	190
191	192	193	194	195	196	197	198	199	200
201	202	203	204	205	206	207	208	209	210
211	212	213	214	215	216	217	218	219	220
221	222	223	224	225	226	227	228	229	230
231	232	233	234	235	236	237	238	239	240
241	242	243	244	245	246	247	248	249	250
251	252	253	254	255	256	257	258	259	260
261	262	263	264	265	266	267	268	269	270
271	272	273	274	275	276	277	278	279	280
281	282	283	284	285	286	287	288	289	290
291	292	293	294	295	296	297	298	299	300

Name Date

Practice Page C

Find three numbers that fit each clue.

1. If you count by this number, you will say 36, but you will not say 40.

2. If you count by this number, you will say 120, but you will not say 130.

3. If you count by this number, you will say 66, but you will not say 77.

Name Date

Practice Page D

Find three numbers that fit each clue.

1. If you count by this number, you will say 56, but you will not say 58.

2. If you count by this number, you will say 300, but you will not say 250.

3. If you count by this number, you will say 100, but you will not say 60.